SRA Reading Mastery
Signature Edition

Curriculum-Based Assessment and Fluency Teacher Handbook
Grade 3

Siegfried Engelmann
Susan Hanner

SRA

Columbus, OH

SRAonline.com

 SRA

Send all inquiries to this address:
SRA/McGraw-Hill
8787 Orion Place
Columbus, OH 43240-4027

ISBN: 978-0-07-612590-6
MHID: 0-07-612590-4

6 7 8 9 10 11 GLO 16 15 14 13

Contents

Introduction

This curriculum-based assessment and fluency system for *Reading Mastery Signature Edition,* Grade 3, is a complete system for monitoring student performance in the program. By using the curriculum-based assessment and fluency system, you can

- ensure that students are properly placed in the program
- measure student achievement within the program
- identify the skills that students have mastered
- maintain individual and group records
- administer remedial exercises

The materials for the curriculum-based assessment and fluency system consist of this Handbook and a separate Student Book for each student. The Student Book contains a placement test and a series of assessments. The Handbook contains instructions for administering the assessments and fluency checkouts, passages for fluency checkouts, remedial exercises for each assessment, Individual Skills Profile Charts, Assessment Group Summary Charts, and an Individual Fluency: Rate/Accuracy Chart.

The Assessments

Two kinds of assessments are used in the curriculum-based assessment and fluency system: the placement test and the mastery tests. The placement test appears on the first page of the Student Book. It measures the decoding and comprehension skills of students entering *Reading Mastery Signature Edition,* Grade 3. The test results provide guidelines for grouping the students and also allow you to identify those students who should not be placed in the program.

The mastery tests are criterion referenced, which means they assess each student's achievement within the program. Each mastery test item measures student mastery of a specific skill or concept taught in *Reading Mastery Signature Edition, Grade 3.* There are seven mastery tests, one for every twenty lessons. The mastery tests measure comprehension, literary appreciation, and study skills.

There are also in-program mastery tests that occur every 10 lessons beginning with lesson 10. These tests consist primarily of content introduced and practiced in the preceding nine lessons. The tests also assess skill items and the vocabulary sentences that students have practiced. Directions for these tests are located in the teacher presentation books. The tests are located in the student textbooks.

Decoding skills are measured by the individual fluency checkouts. Beginning with lesson 10, each student receives an individual reading fluency checkout every fifth lesson. For these individual fluency checkouts, a student reads a passage aloud as you count decoding errors. A fluency checkout takes about a minute and a half per student. The fluency checkout passages, along with further instructions, begin on page 31.

The Remedial Exercises

To pass each mastery test, a student must answer at least 80 percent of the items correctly. The remedial exercises are designed to help students who score below 80 percent on the assessments. Each assessment has its own set of remedial exercises. The exercises provide a general review of the tested skills and concepts, using examples different from those on the test. There is a specific remedial exercise for every tested skill or concept. The remedial exercises are similar to the exercises found in the Presentation Books for *Reading Mastery Signature Edition,* Grade 3.

The Charts

Three charts are used in the curriculum-based assessment and fluency system: the Individual Skills Profile Chart, the Group Summary Chart and the Individual Fluency: Rate/Accuracy Chart.

The Individual Skills Profile Chart appears on page 58 of this Teacher Handbook. This chart lists the specific skills and concepts taught in *Reading Mastery Signature Edition,* Grade 3, and indicates what each assessment item measures. When the chart is completed, it will show how well a student has mastered the skills and concepts taught in *Reading Mastery Signature Edition,* Grade 3.

The Group Summary Chart appears on page 59. It summarizes the group's scores on the assessments. The chart provides an objective measure of the group's progress and can be used to evaluate the group's overall performance.

The Individual Fluency: Rate/Accuracy Chart appears on pages 60 and 61. This chart helps you keep track of an individual student's fluency checkout scores.

Use of Color, Bold, and Italic Type

Text is distinguished in the following ways for your convenience in administering the test and presenting remedial exercises.
- Blue text shows what you say.
- **Bold blue text shows words you stress.**
- (Text in parentheses tells what you do.)
- *Italic text gives students' responses.* (If a student response is preceded by the word *Idea,* the printed response gives the general idea of a correct answer.)

Placement Test

A reproducible copy of the placement test appears on page 62. The placement test has two parts. Part 1 consists of five vocabulary words and a reading passage. The vocabulary word-reading is not scored, but the reading passage is both timed and scored.

Part 1 is administered individually and requires about three minutes per student. Each student will need a Student Book, and you will need a **stop watch.**

Part 2 may be presented to all students at the same time. For Part 2, students write answers to comprehension questions about the Part 1 passage. Students have two minutes to complete Part 2.

Instructions for Part 1

Administer Part 1 in a corner of the classroom, so that other students will not overhear the testing. Use the following script.

Vocabulary Reading

1. (Give a Student Book to the student.)
- Open the Student Book to page 1. ✔
2. (Point to the column of words at the top of Part 1.)

(Teacher reference)

1. California
2. Pacific
3. loudspeaker
4. lifeboat
5. Japan

---

3. Touch word 1. ✔
- That word is **California.**
4. (Repeat step 3 for words 2-5.)
5. Your turn to read those words.
6. Word 1. What word? *California.*
7. (Repeat step 6 for words 2–5.)

Passage Reading

1. (Point to the passage in part 1.)
- You're going to read this passage out loud. I want you to read it as well as you can. Don't try to read it so fast that you make mistakes. But don't read it so slowly that it doesn't make any sense. You have two minutes to read the passage. Go.

2. (Time the student. If the student takes more than three seconds on a word, say the word, count it as an error, and permit the student to continue reading. To record errors, make one tally mark for each error. Count all the following behaviors as errors:)
- Misreading a word [count as one error].
- Omitting a word part [count as one error].
- Sounding out a word but not saying the word at a normal speaking rate [count as one error].
- Skipping a word [count as one error].
- Skipping a line [immediately show the student the correct line; count as one error].
- Not identifying a word within three seconds [tell the word; count as one error].
- Reading a word incorrectly and then reading it correctly [count as one error].
- Also count each word not read by the end of the two-minute limit as an error. For example, if the student is eight words from the end of the passage by the time limit, count eight errors.

3. (Collect the Student Book.)

Instructions for Part 2

After you've administered Part 1 to all the students, present part 2, which is a group test. Administer Part 2 no more than two hours after students complete Part 1. Use the following script:

Comprehension Questions

1. (Assemble the students.)
2. (Give a Student Book to each student.)
3. Open your Student Book to page 1 and touch Part 2. ✔
- These are questions about the passage you read earlier. Write the answers. You have two minutes to finish. Go.
4. (Time the students. Collect the Student Books after two minutes.)
5. (Check the tests using the following Answer Key.)

Answer Key

1. Idea: Because the ship was on fire
2. Idea: Linda, Kathy
3. lifeboats
4. Linda
5. 13
6. 10
7. hand
8. Idea: In a lifeboat
9. Japan
10. Idea: To see their father
11. 3 days

Placement Criteria

Use the table below to determine placement for each student.

Errors	Placement
If a student makes seven or more errors on Part 1 **OR** three or more errors on part 2	Place the student in a more elementary reading program, such as *Reading Mastery Signature Edition, Grade 2.*
If a student makes no more than six errors on Part 1 **AND** no more than one error on Part 2	Place the student in *Reading Mastery Signature Edition, Grade 3,* lesson 1.

If you suspect that some students are too advanced for the program (students who score 0 or 1 on the placement test and who exhibit good comprehension skills), present the main story from lesson 103 to them. Present the tasks specified for the main story oral reading, and assign items 1–10 from lesson 103 in the workbook.

If the student makes no more than eight story-reading errors and no more than two workbook errors on lesson 103, place the student in a higher-level program, such as *Reading Mastery Signature Edition, Grade 4.*

Remedies

Students' performance on the Placement Test shows whether they are weak in decoding, comprehension, or both. Their performance may also imply remedies.

If students fail part 1, they are weak in decoding. The simplest remedy for these students is to select material that they are able to read without making more than two errors per hundred words. Set a rate criterion for these students (based on their current rate for reading one hundred words with no more than two errors). As students improve, change the criterion so students are required to read faster. Continue to provide ample practice until the students read at the minimum rate of 90 words per minute without making more than two errors per hundred words.

If students fail part 2, they are weak in comprehension. Give them practice on basic comprehension questions (who, what, when, where, why). Direct these students to read a passage aloud. Ask questions after each sentence. Make sure that each question can be clearly answered by the passage. Provide this kind of comprehension practice until the students are proficient at answering questions.

Retesting

When you feel that students are firm on skills that were initially deficient, readminister the Placement Test. If students fail a second time, they should be placed, if possible, in a more elementary program, such as *Reading Mastery Signature Edition, Grade 2.*

Assessments

Lesson 20

Administering the Assessment

The Lesson 20 Assessment should be administered after the students complete all work on lesson 20 and before they begin work on lesson 21. To administer the assessment, you will need a Student Book and a pencil for each student. Use the following script.

1. (Have the students clear their desks and make sure each student has a pencil.)

2. You're going to take a test in your Student Book. I will give each of you a Student Book. Do not open the book until I tell you.

3. (Pass out the Student Books.)

4. Find the **Lesson 20** test in your Student Book. ✔
- This is the first test. For each item, you must circle the letter of the correct answer. There is no time limit.
- When you are finished, close your Student Book and look up at me. Begin the test now.

Grading the Assessment

You can grade the tests yourself, or the students can grade their own tests. If the students grade their own tests, use the following script.

1. We're going to grade the test. I'll read the correct answer for each item.
- If the answer is correct, mark it with a **C.**
- If the answer is wrong, mark it with an **X.**

2. (Read the correct answers from the answer key.)

3. Count up the number of correct answers and enter the score at the bottom of the test. ✔

Answer Key

Lesson 20

For each item, circle the letter of the correct answer.

1. In which direction do geese migrate in the fall?
   - (a.) South
   - b. West
   - c. North

2. How long does it take for the earth to go all the way around the sun?
   - a. One day
   - b. One month
   - (c.) One year

3. What is the fattest part of the earth called?
   - (a.) Equator
   - b. North Pole
   - c. Tilt

4. What word means the opposite of *careful*?
   - (a.) Careless
   - b. Carefully
   - c. Caring

5. What season is it when the North Pole leans away from the sun?
   - (a.) Winter
   - b. Spring
   - c. Summer

6. In what season are polar bears the most dangerous?
   - a. Winter
   - (b.) Spring
   - c. Summer

7. In which state did Henry and the other geese spend the winter?
   - (a.) Florida
   - b. Michigan
   - c. Kentucky

8. Pretend you are on an ice chunk in the middle of the ocean. The wind starts blowing from the south. In which direction will the ice chunk move?
   - (a.) North
   - b. South
   - c. East

Look at the map below. Then answer items 9–10.

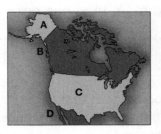

9. What is the name of country C?
   - a. Mexico
   - b. Canada
   - (c.) United States

10. To which country does state A belong?
   - a. Mexico
   - b. Canada
   - (c.) United States

Read the passage below. Then answer items 11–16.

During the winter in Alaska, parts of the ocean are covered with very thick ice. In some places, the ice is three meters thick. During the winter, you can walk far out on the frozen ocean. Then the spring comes, and the ice starts to melt. When it melts, chunks of ice break off and float into the ocean. Some of these chunks are as big as a schoolyard. Some are no bigger than a table.

When an ice floe begins to break up in the spring, you can hear it. At night, as you lie in your summer home, you can hear many sounds. You can hear the sound of wolves and sometimes bears growling. You can hear a million buzzes from a million bugs that circle above you. You can hear the occasional bark of the seals. And you can hear the ice floe. It moans and groans. It creaks and it cracks. Sometimes, it squeaks and squeals.

Ice floes also make noise in the winter. The ice floes creak and groan when the air is so cold that sweat freezes to your face. They are so cold that a deep breath hurts and makes you cough.

In the winter, the ice floes creak and groan because great sheets of ice are crowding together and there is not enough room for them. So the ice floes buckle. Sometimes, great chunks of ice break off and are pushed over other chunks. The chunks make noise when they move around.

11. Which animals can you hear barking?
   - (a.) Seals
   - b. Wolves
   - c. Bears

12. Why do the ice floes make noise in the winter?
   - a. The ice is melting.
   - b. The ice is breaking off and floating into the ocean.
   - (c.) Sheets of ice are crowding together.

13. When can you walk far out on the ocean?
   - a. During the spring
   - (b.) During the winter
   - c. During the summer

14. How is the spring ice floe different from the winter ice floe?
   - a. The spring ice floe makes noise.
   - b. The spring ice floe is in Alaska.
   - (c.) The spring ice floe is melting.

15. Why does the ice floe begin to break up in the spring?
   - a. The animals break it to pieces.
   - (b.) The weather is warmer.
   - c. The water gets colder.

16. What probably happens to the ice floe in the summer?
   - (a.) It disappears.
   - b. It gets larger.
   - c. It turns into snow.

STOP - end of test - SCORE: _____

Recording Individual Results

The students record their test results on the Individual Skills Profile Chart. Use the following script to explain the chart.

1. (Give each student a copy of the chart on page 58.)

2. Touch the left side of the chart. ✔
- The words on the left side tell about the reading skills you are learning.

3. Touch the top line of the chart. ✔
- The numbers on the top line are lesson numbers.
- Everybody, what is the first number? (Signal.) *20.*
- What is the last number? (Signal.) *140.*
- You will take a test on each of those lessons. You have just finished the test for lesson 20.

4. Touch the column of numbers under lesson 20. ✔
- Those numbers tell about the items on the test for lesson 20.
- Everybody, what is the first number in the column? (Signal.) *11.*
- That number tells about item 11 on the test.
- Now look down the column. What is the last number in the column? (Signal.) *8.*
- What item does that number tell about? (Signal.) *Item 8.*
- You can see that the order of the numbers changes in each column.

5. Here's how you record your test results on the chart. First look at the test and find out which items you got wrong. Then circle those items on the chart.
- Which number would you circle if you got item 2 wrong? (Signal.) *2.*

6. Now record your results. I will help you if you have any questions. (Circulate among the students as they record their results.)

7. (After the students finish, say:) Now count up the items that you did **not** circle and write the total in the **Total** box near the bottom of the column. The total should be the same as your test score.

8. Below the **Total** box is the **Retest** box. If you scored 0 to 12 points, write an **X** in the **Retest** box.

- Below the **Retest** box is the **Final Score** box. If you scored 13 to 16 points, write your score in the **Final Score** box.

Remedial Exercises

Students who scored 0 to 12 points on the test should be given remedial help. After the regular reading period is over, assemble these students and present the following exercises. The students will need their Student Books.

EXERCISE 1   General Review

1. In what season do geese fly back to their homes in Canada? (Call on a student. Idea: *Spring.*)
- In which direction do they fly? (Call on a student. Idea: *North.*)

2. How often does the earth circle the sun? (Call on a student. Idea: *Once a year.*)

3. What is the North Pole? (Call on a student. Idea: *The top of the earth.*)
- What is the equator? (Call on a student. Idea: *The fattest part of the earth.*)

4. When you are **careless,** how do you act? (Call on a student. Idea: *Without care.*)

5. Everybody, what season is it when the North Pole leans toward the sun? (Signal.) *Summer.*
- Everybody, what season is it when the North Pole leans away from the sun? (Signal.) *Winter.*

6. What kind of bear was Usk? (Call on a student. Idea: *A polar bear.*)
- In what season was Usk the most dangerous? (Call on a student. Idea: *Spring.*)

7. What were some of the states that Old Henry the goose visited when he flew south? (Call on individual students. Ideas: *Michigan, Kentucky, Georgia, Florida.*)

8. Everybody, if the wind is blowing from the east, which direction is it blowing toward? (Signal.) *West.*
- So if a wind blows from the east, in which direction will it blow things? (Signal.) *West.*

9. Everybody, find the map on page 2 of your Student Book. ✔
   - What's the name of state A? (Signal.) *Alaska.*
   - Get ready to tell me the letter for each country I name.
   - Canada. (Signal.) *B.*
   - United States. (Signal.) *C.*
   - Mexico. (Signal.) *D.*

EXERCISE 2   Passage Reading

---

1. Everybody, find the passage on page 3 of your Student Book. ✔
   - You're going to read the passage out loud.

2. (Call on individual students to read several sentences each. Correct all decoding errors. When the students finish, present the following questions.)

3. What noise do the wolves make? (Call on a student. Idea: *Howling.*)
   - What noise do the bears make? (Call on a student. Idea: *Growling.*)
   - What noise do the seals make? (Call on a student. Idea: *Barking.*)

4. In what season is the ice floe the largest? (Call on a student. Idea: *In the winter.*)
   - What happens to the weather in the spring? (Call on a student. Idea: *It gets warmer.*)
   - So what happens to the ice floe? (Call on individual students. Ideas: *It melts; it gets smaller.*)

5. In the winter, the sheets of ice are crowding together. So what happens to some of them? (Call on individual students. Ideas: *They break; they buckle.*)

Retesting the Students

After you have completed the remedial exercises, retest each student individually. To administer the retest, you will need the student's Student Book, a blank copy of the Student Book, and a red pencil. Test the student in a corner of the classroom, so that the other students will not overhear the testing. Give the student the blank copy of the Student Book. Say, Open the book to lesson 20. You're going to take this test again. Read each item aloud and tell me the answer.

Use the student's own Student Book to grade the retest. With the red pencil, mark each correct answer with a **C** and each incorrect answer with an **X.** Then count one point for each correct answer and write the new score at the bottom of the page. Finally, revise the Individual Skills Profile Chart by drawing an **X** over any items the student missed on the retest. The chart should now show which items the student missed on the initial test and which items the student missed on the retest.

Page 57 of this Teacher Handbook shows a sample Individual Skills Profile Chart.

Recording Group Results

After the students have completely filled in the Individual Skills Profile Chart for lesson 20, you should fill in the Group Summary Chart, which appears on page 59 of this Teacher Handbook. Make a copy of the chart; then enter the students' names on the left side of the chart. Record the students' scores in the boxes under the appropriate lesson number.

Fluency: Rate/Accuracy

Administer the fluency checkout for lesson 20. For further instructions, see page 29.

Tested Skills and Concepts

The Lesson 20 Assessment measures student mastery of the following skills.
- answering literal questions (item 11)
- comprehending vocabulary definitions (items 3–4)
- distinguishing settings by features (item 7)
- identifying literal cause and effect (item 12)
- identifying standard measurements (item 2)
- inferring causes and effects (item 15)
- interpreting maps (items 9–10)
- making comparisons (item 14)
- making predictions (item 16)
- memorizing science facts and rules (items 5–6)
- recalling details and events (item 1)
- sequencing events (item 13)
- using rules to predict outcomes (item 8)

Lesson 40

Administering the Assessment

The Lesson 40 Assessment should be administered after the students complete all work on lesson 40 and before they begin work on lesson 41. To administer the assessment, you will need a Student Book and a pencil for each student. Use the following script.

1. (Have the students clear their desks and make sure that each student has a pencil.)

2. You're going to take another test in your Student Book. Do not open the book until I tell you.

3. (Pass out the Student Books.)

4. Find the test for Lesson 40. ✔
- Answer all the items on the test. For each item, circle the letter of the correct answer.
- There is no time limit. When you are finished, close your Student Book and look up at me. Begin the test now.

Grading the Assessment

You can grade the tests yourself, or the students can grade their own tests. If the students grade their own tests, use the following script.

1. We're going to grade the test. I'll read the correct answer for each item.
- If the answer is correct, mark it with a **C.**
- If the answer is wrong, mark it with an **X.**

2. (Read the correct answers from the answer key.)

3. Count up the number of correct answers and enter the score at the bottom of the test. ✔

Answer Key

Lesson 40

For each item, circle the letter of the correct answer.

1. Which one of the following animals came last on Earth?
   a. Strange sea animals
   b. Cows
   c. Dinosaurs

2. What do we call a person who makes an object for the first time?
   a. Soldier
   b. Inventor
   c. Engineer

3. Which dinosaur was a huge killer?
   a. Triceratops
   b. Tyrannosaurus
   c. Torontosaurus

4. Which one of the following things is made by humans?
   a. Roads
   b. Dirt
   c. Roses

5. What do inventors do when they see a need?
   a. Try to forget about the need
   b. Try to invent another need
   c. Figure out how to meet the need

Look at the picture below. Then answer items 6–9.

6. Which layer went into the pile first?
   a. E
   b. G
   c. H

7. In which layer will you find the skeletons of horses?
   a. E
   b. F
   c. G

8. Which layer shows the Mesozoic era?
   a. E
   b. F
   c. G

9. How is layer F different from layer G?
   a. Layer F came earlier
   b. Layer F is under the ground
   c. Layer F came later

Look at the picture below. Then answer item 10.

10. How many times did the hailstone go through a cloud?
    a. One time
    b. Two times
    c. Three times

Read the passage below. Then answer items 11–16.

Edna and Carla were on a lifeboat in the middle of the ocean. Edna looked over the side of the boat into the water. It was very dark blue. She could see some fish swimming around beneath the boat. They seemed to like staying in the shadow of the boat.

As Edna looked at the fish, she remembered something she had once read. Fish have a lot of fresh water in them. If you chew on raw fish, you can squeeze the water out. Edna didn't like the idea of chewing on raw fish, but she knew that without water, she and Carla would not last for more than a few hours in the hot sun.

Edna moved to the front of the boat and started to look for fishing gear. But then she noticed a slim line of smoke in the distance. It was the kind of smoke that ships make. "A ship!" Edna shouted as she stood up. "I think there's a ship over there." She pointed.

The next hour seemed longer than any hour Edna ever remembered. Edna didn't do anything but watch the approaching ship. She felt that if she stopped watching it, it would disappear.

11. Why did Edna want to chew on raw fish?
    a. She liked the taste.
    b. She needed water.
    c. She was hungry.

12. Why do you think the fish liked to stay in the shadow of the boat?
    a. It was cool in the shadow.
    b. They could hide from the girls.
    c. It was warm in the shadow.

13. Why was Edna so excited when she saw the ship?
    a. She thought it would rescue them.
    b. She was afraid it would hit them.
    c. She thought it was on fire.

14. What would Edna probably do if the ship turned away?
    a. Take a nap
    b. Go swimming
    c. Signal the ship

15. Around what time of day does this story take place?
    a. Dawn
    b. Midnight
    c. Noon

16. How did Edna first know that a ship was approaching?
    a. She saw some smoke.
    b. She saw the ship.
    c. She heard the ship's horn.

STOP - end of test - SCORE: _____

Recording Individual Results

Use the following script to record individual results.

1. (Distribute the Individual Skills Profile Charts.)

2. You're going to record your test results for lesson 40.
- First look at the test and find out which items you got wrong. Then circle those items on the chart. I will help you if you have any questions. (Circulate among the students as they record their results.)

3. (After the students finish, say:) Count up the items that you did **not** circle and write the total in the **Total** box near the bottom of the column. The total should be the same as your test score. ✔

4. Now you'll fill in the other boxes for lesson 40.
- If you scored 0 to 12 points, write an **X** in the **Retest** box.
- If you scored 13 to 16 points, write your score in the **Final Score** box.

Remedial Exercises

Students who scored 0 to 12 points on the test should be given remedial help. After the regular reading period is over, assemble these students and present the following exercises. The students will need their Student Books.

EXERCISE 1   General Review
---

1. You learned about two dinosaurs: Triceratops and Tyrannosaurus.
- Which dinosaur had horns and armor? (Signal.) *Triceratops.*
- Which dinosaur was a huge killer? (Signal.) *Tyrannosaurus.*

2. Name some things that are made by humans. (Call on individual students. Ideas: *Cars, radios, roads, houses.*)
- Name some things that are **not** made by humans. (Call on individual students. Ideas: *Trees, rocks, rivers, mountains.*)

3. The electric light was an invention. So what kind of person made the first electric light? (Call on a student. Idea: *An inventor.*)
- If people need a better mousetrap, what will an inventor try to do? (Call on individual students. Ideas: *Invent a better mousetrap; meet the need.*)

4. If a hailstone has five rings, how many times has it gone through a cloud? (Call on a student. Idea: *Five times.*)

5. Everybody, find the picture on page 4 of your Student Book. ✔
- Which layer went into the pile last? (Signal.) *E.*
- Which layer shows the Mesozoic era? (Signal.) *F.*
- In which layer will you find the skeletons of strange sea animals? (Signal.) *G.*
- In which layer will you find the skeletons of dinosaurs? (Signal.) *F.*
- In which layer will you find the skeletons of goats? (Signal.) *E.*

EXERCISE 2   Passage Reading
---

1. Find the passage on page 5 of your Student Book. ✔
- You're going to read the passage out loud.

2. (Call on individual students to read several sentences each. Correct all decoding errors. When the students finish, present the following questions.)

3. How did Edna think she could get some water? (Call on a student. Idea: *By chewing on raw fish.*)

4. Fish do not like being in hot water. So where would a fish rather be, in a shady pond or a sunny pond? (Call on a student. Idea: *A shady pond.*)

5. What did Edna realize when she saw the smoke? (Call on a student. Idea: *A ship was approaching.*)
- How could the ship help Edna and Carla? (Call on a student. Idea: *It could rescue them.*)

6. The story says the sun was hot. At what time of day is the sun the hottest? (Call on individual students. Ideas: *Noon; early afternoon.*)

Retesting the Students

After you have completed the remedial exercises, retest each student individually. To administer the retest, you will need the student's Student Book, a blank copy of the Student Book, and a red pencil. Test the student in a corner of the classroom, so that the other students will not overhear the testing. Give the student the blank copy of the Student Book. Say, Open the book to lesson 40. You're going to take this test again. Read each item aloud and tell me the answer.

Use the student's own Student Book to grade the retest. With the red pencil, mark each correct answer with a **C** and each incorrect answer with an **X.** Then count one point for each correct answer and write the new score at the bottom of the page. Finally, revise the Individual Skills Profile Chart by drawing an **X** over any items the student missed on the retest. The chart should now show which items the student missed on the initial test and which items the student missed on the retest.

All of the Individual Skills Profile Charts should now be completely filled in for lesson 40. Enter the students' final scores in the appropriate boxes on the Group Summary Chart.

Fluency: Rate/Accuracy

Administer the fluency checkout for lesson 40. For instructions, see page 29.

Tested Skills and Concepts

The Lesson 40 Assessment measures student mastery of the following skills.

- comprehending vocabulary definitions (items 2–3)
- drawing conclusions (item 10)
- evaluating problems and solutions (item 5)
- inferring a character's point of view (item 16)
- inferring causes and effects (item 12)
- inferring story details and events (item 15)
- interpreting a character's feelings (item 13)
- interpreting a character's motives (item 11)
- interpreting diagrams (item 6)
- making comparisons (item 9)
- memorizing science facts and rules (items 7–8)
- predicting a character's actions (item 14)
- sequencing events (item 1)
- using rules to classify objects (item 4)

Lesson 60

Administering the Assessment

The Lesson 60 Assessment should be administered after the students complete all work on lesson 60 and before they begin work on lesson 61. To administer the assessment, you will need a Student Book and a pencil for each student. Use the following script.

1. (Have the students clear their desks and make sure that each student has a pencil.)

2. You're going to take another test in your Student Book. Do not open the book until I tell you.

3. (Pass out the Student Books.)

4. Find the test for Lesson 60. ✔
- Answer all the items on the test. For each item, circle the letter of the correct answer.
- There is no time limit. When you are finished, close your Student Book and look up at me. Begin the test now.

Grading the Assessment

You can grade the tests yourself, or the students can grade their own tests. If the students grade their own tests, use the following script.

1. We're going to grade the test. I'll read the correct answer for each item.
- If the answer is correct, mark it with a **C.**
- If the answer is wrong, mark it with an **X.**

2. (Read the correct answers from the answer key.)

3. Count up the number of correct answers and enter the score at the bottom of the test. ✔

Answer Key

Lesson 60

For each item, circle the letter of the correct answer.

1. What do we call businesses that make things?
   a. Inventors
   b. Lawyers
   c. Manufacturers ⭕

2. What does *purchase* mean?
   a. Buy ⭕
   b. Sell
   c. Rent

3. What does an inventor do with a problem?
   a. Tries to ignore it
   b. Tries to find a need
   c. Tries to solve it ⭕

4. How many beams of light did Leonard use in his invention?
   a. Two ⭕
   b. One
   c. Four

5. What is the largest planet?
   a. Neptune
   b. Saturn
   c. Jupiter ⭕

6. Which planet is closest to the sun?
   a. Earth
   b. Mercury ⭕
   c. Venus

Look at the time line below. Then answer items 7–8.

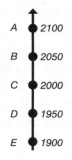

A — 2100
B — 2050
C — 2000
D — 1950
E — 1900

7. Which years are in the future?
   a. A and B ⭕
   b. C and D
   c. A and E

8. Which year came first?
   a. A
   b. C
   c. E ⭕

Look at the map below. Then answer items 9–10.

9. What is the name of country A?
   a. Canada
   b. Japan ⭕
   c. Mexico

10. What is the name of the ocean between country A and country B?
    a. Atlantic Ocean
    b. Pacific Ocean ⭕
    c. Indian Ocean

Read the passage below. Then answer items 11–16.

From the space station, Wendy could see the city of Tokyo, the largest city in Japan. The space station was about twenty miles from Tokyo. Wendy stood in front of the large window and looked down at the beautiful city. She had traveled by jet from Canada to Japan. She had landed at the Tokyo airport. Five other students who were going on the trip to Jupiter were on Wendy's flight. Newspaper reporters met the students at the Tokyo airport. They questioned the students about how they felt about being selected to go on this trip. Wendy said that it was the most important thing that had ever happened to her.

At the airport, Wendy and the other students had boarded a special bus that took them from the airport to the space station. As Wendy looked out the window, she wondered if she had packed everything she would need on the trip. Part of the letter that told her that she had been selected was a list of things that she should take with her. The list named things like toothbrush and clothing. Part of the list was underlined: "Your baggage must not weigh more than 100 pounds."

Wendy had her camera, three books, paper, and pencils. She didn't have room for her computer and some of the other things she had wanted to take. In fact, before she packed, she had her room filled with things that she wanted to take. But she had to leave most of them behind.

11. When does this story take place?
    a. In the present
    b. In the future ⭕
    c. In the past

12. Why did Wendy leave her computer behind?
    a. Computers weren't allowed on the trip.
    b. She didn't have room in her baggage. ⭕
    c. She forgot about her computer.

13. What was the first thing Wendy did?
    a. Traveled from Canada to Japan ⭕
    b. Traveled from Tokyo to the space station
    c. Landed in Tokyo

14. Where will Wendy probably travel next?
    a. Tokyo
    b. Canada
    c. Jupiter ⭕

15. How did Wendy feel about being selected for the trip?
    a. Sad
    b. Jealous
    c. Proud ⭕

16. Which one of the following things was probably on the list that Wendy received?
    a. Shoes ⭕
    b. Baseball glove
    c. Chair

STOP - end of test - SCORE: _____

Recording Individual Results

Use the following script to record individual results.

1. (Distribute the Individual Skills Profile Chart.)

2. You're going to record your test results for lesson 60.
   - First look at the test and find out which items you got wrong. Then circle those items on the chart. I will help you if you have any questions. (Circulate among the students as they record their results.)

3. (After the students finish, say:) Count up the items that you did **not** circle and write the total in the **Total** box near the bottom of the column. The total should be the same as your test score. ✔

4. Now you'll fill in the other boxes for lesson 60.
   - If you scored 0 to 12 points, write an **X** in the **Retest** box.
   - If you scored 13 to 16 points, write your score in the **Final Score** box.

Remedial Exercises

Students who scored 0 to 12 points on the test should be given remedial help. After the regular reading period is over, assemble these students and present the following exercises. The students will need their Student Books.

EXERCISE 1   General Review

1. What does an inventor do? (Call on individual students. Ideas: *Invents things; makes something for the first time.*)
   - What does a manufacturer do? (Call on individual students. Ideas: *Manufactures things; makes products.*)

2. What did Leonard do each time he ran into a problem with his invention? (Call on a student. Idea: *Tried to solve the problem.*)

3. Listen to this sentence: They want to buy a loaf of bread.
   - Say that sentence with another word for **buy.** (Call on a student. Idea: *They want to purchase a loaf of bread.*)

4. Everybody, find the time line on page 6 of your Student Book. ✔
   - Get ready to tell me if each year is in the **future** or the **past.**
   - Year B. (Signal.) *Future.*
   - Year D. (Signal.) *Past.*
   - Year C. (Signal.) *Past.*

5. Which year came first, B or D? (Signal.) *D.*

6. Find the map on page 7. ✔
   - Everybody, what's the name of country A? (Signal.) *Japan.*
   - What's the name of country B? (Signal.) *Canada.*
   - What's the name of country C? (Signal.) *United States.*
   - Where is the Pacific Ocean? (Call on a student. Idea: *Between Japan and the United States and Canada.*)

EXERCISE 2   Passage Reading

1. Everybody, find the passage on page 7 of your Student Book. ✔
   - You're going to read the passage out loud.

2. (Call on individual students to read several sentences each. Correct all decoding errors. When the students finish, present the following questions.)

3. When will people fly to Jupiter? (Call on a student. Idea: *In the future.*)

4. Why did Wendy have to leave so many things behind after she packed her bags? (Call on a student. Idea: *Her bags were full.*)

5. In which country had Wendy started her trip? (Call on a student. Idea: *Canada.*)
   - Where did Wendy go after she landed at the airport? (Call on a student. Idea: *To the space station.*)

6. Where will Wendy be going after she leaves the space station? (Call on a student. Idea: *Jupiter.*)

7. The list said that Wendy should bring important things like a toothbrush and clothing. Name some other things that were probably on the list. (Call on individual students. Ideas: *Shoes; soap; flashlight.*)

8. How would you feel if someone selected you to go on an important trip? (Call on individual students. Ideas: *Proud; excited; happy.*)

- So how do you think Wendy feels? (Call on individual students. Ideas: *The same; proud; excited; happy.*)

Retesting the Students

After you have completed the remedial exercises, retest each student individually. To administer the retest, you will need the student's Student Book, a blank copy of the Student Book, and a red pencil. Test the student in a corner of the classroom, so that the other students will not overhear the testing. Give the student the blank copy of the Student Book. Say, Open the book to lesson 60. You're going to take this test again. Read each item aloud and tell me the answer.

Use the student's own Student Book to grade the retest. With the red pencil, mark each correct answer with a **C** and each incorrect answer with an **X.** Then count one point for each correct answer and write the new score at the bottom of the page. Finally, revise the Individual Skills Profile Chart by drawing an **X** over any items the student missed on the retest. The chart should now show which items the student missed on the initial test and which items the student missed on the retest.

All of the Individual Skills Profile Charts should now be completely filled in for lesson 60. Enter the students' final scores in the appropriate boxes on the Group Summary Chart.

Fluency: Rate/Accuracy

Administer the fluency checkout for lesson 60. For further instructions, see page 29.

Tested Skills and Concepts

The Lesson 60 Assessment measures student mastery of the following skills.

- comprehending vocabulary definitions (items 1–2)
- drawing conclusions (item 16)
- evaluating problems and solutions (item 3)
- identifying literal cause and effect (item 12)
- inferring story details and events (item 11)
- interpreting a character's feelings (item 15)
- interpreting maps (item 9–10)
- interpreting time lines (item 7–8)
- making predictions (item 14)
- memorizing science facts and rules (items 5–6)
- recalling details and events (item 4)
- sequencing events (item 13)

Lesson 80

Administering the Assessment

The Lesson 80 Assessment should be administered after the students complete all work on lesson 80 and before they begin work on lesson 81. To administer the assessment, you will need a Student Book and a pencil for each student. Use the following script.

1. (Have the students clear their desks and make sure that each student has a pencil.)

2. You're going to take another test in your Student Book. Do not open the book until I tell you.

3. (Pass out the Student Books.)

4. Find the test for Lesson 80. ✔
   - Answer all the items on the test. For each item, circle the letter of the correct answer.
   - There is no time limit. When you are finished, close your Student Book and look up at me. Begin the test now.

Grading the Assessment

You can grade the tests yourself, or the students can grade their own tests. If the students grade their own tests, use the following script.

1. We're going to grade the test. I'll read the correct answer for each item.
   - If the answer is correct, mark it with a **C.**
   - If the answer is wrong, mark it with an **X.**

2. (Read the correct answers from the answer key.)

3. Count up the number of correct answers and enter the score at the bottom of the test. ✔

Answer Key

Lesson 80

For items 1–2, circle the letter of the answer that means the same thing as the underlined word.

1. The loud noise <u>bothered</u> the sleeping cats.
   a. deserved
   b. (disturbed)
   c. managed

2. Everyone agreed that Yvonne's singing was <u>wonderful</u>.
   a. (fantastic)
   b. pale
   c. ridiculous

For items 3–16, circle the letter of the correct answer.

3. What do we call the people who watch an event?
   a. performers
   b. (audience)
   c. radiance

4. How is Colorado different from Utah?
   a. Colorado has mountains.
   b. Colorado is a state.
   c. (Colorado is further east.)

5. When you teach a dog a simple trick, when do you reward the dog?
   a. (When the dog does the trick)
   b. When the dog tries to do the trick
   c. When the dog gets hungry

6. Which planet has the most gravity?
   a. (Jupiter)
   b. Earth
   c. Neptune

7. On which planet could you jump the highest?
   a. Jupiter
   b. (Earth)
   c. Neptune

8. Why can't you breathe on Io?
   a. (It has no oxygen.)
   b. It has no gravity.
   c. It is too far from the sun.

9. What is another name for hot, melted rock?
   a. volcano
   b. (lava)
   c. granite

Look at the picture below. Then answer item 10.

A B C

10. Which glass will make the lowest ring?
    a. A
    b. (B)
    c. C

Read the passage below. Then answer items 11–16.

Maria Sanchez stood in the kitchen of her pet shop and watched Waldo pour different things that he had cooked into a big bowl. She couldn't believe what was happening. Birds and squirrels were looking in the window. Dogs and cats were running around outside the window. The animals in the pet shop were howling and screeching and jumping around.

"What makes the animals act that way?" Maria asked Waldo.

Waldo smiled and looked up from his cooking. "My food," he said. "It's very good."

Maria dipped her spoon into the bowl, filled it with food, and put it in her mouth. She tried not to make a sour face, but the food tasted bad—very bad. "My," she said, trying to smile, "that certainly has an unusual taste." She wasn't really lying. The food did have an unusual taste—unusually bad.

Waldo finished cooking some corn and rice. He dumped the corn and rice into the bowl with the other things he had cooked. Then he began to whistle. He walked into the pet shop with his food. Maria followed. Waldo began opening the bird cages. "No," Maria shouted. "We'll never be able to catch them."

"They won't fly away," Waldo said. And he was right. The birds landed on his shoulders and on his head. Two of them tried to get into the bowl of food, but he brushed them away with his hand. Those two birds landed on his shoulder and sat there.

Next, Waldo opened all the cat cages. "No," Maria shouted. "They'll go after the birds."

11. Why didn't Maria tell Waldo that the food tasted bad?
    a. The food tasted good to her.
    b. She was afraid of Waldo.
    c. (She didn't want to hurt his feelings.)

12. Why did Waldo think the food was very good?
    a. Because people liked it
    b. (Because the animals liked it)
    c. Because he paid a lot for it

13. What will the cats probably do?
    a. Go after the birds
    b. Leave the store
    c. (Go after the food)

14. Why were the animals howling and screeching?
    a. They were tired of living in cages.
    b. They were in pain.
    c. (They smelled the food.)

15. When did Waldo open the bird cages?
    a. Before he cooked the food
    b. After he opened the cat cages
    c. (Before he opened the cat cages)

16. How did Waldo keep the birds away from the food?
    a. He covered the food.
    b. (He brushed them away with his hand.)
    c. He put the birds in their cages.

STOP - end of test - SCORE:_____

Recording Individual Results

Use the following script to record individual results.

1. (Distribute the Individual Skills Profile Chart.)

2. You're going to record your test results for lesson 80.
   - First look at the test and find out which items you got wrong. Then circle those items on the chart. I will help you if you have any questions. (Circulate among the students as they record their results.)

3. (After the students finish, say:) Count up the items that you did not circle and write the total in the **Total** box near the bottom of the column. The total should be the same as your test score. ✔

4. Now you'll fill in the other boxes for lesson 80.
   - If you scored 0 to 12 points, write an **X** in the **Retest** box.
   - If you scored 13 to 16 points, write your score in the **Final Score** box.

Remedial Exercises

Students who scored 0 to 12 points on the test should be given remedial help. After the regular reading period is over, assemble these students and present the following exercises. The students will need their Student Books.

EXERCISE 1   Vocabulary Review

1. Let's talk about the meanings of some words.

2. The first word is **deserve.** Something you **deserve** is something you should receive.
   - Everybody, what's another way of saying **The students should receive good grades?** (Signal.) *The students deserve good grades.*

3. The next word is **disturb.** When you **disturb** somebody, you bother them.
   - Everybody, what's another way of saying **The bright light bothered the driver?** (Signal.) *The bright light disturbed the driver.*

4. The next word is **manage.** When you **manage** to do something, you work hard until you do it.

- Everybody, what's another way of saying **They worked hard until they fixed the roof?** (Signal.) *They managed to fix the roof.*

5. The next word is **fantastic.** When something is **fantastic,** it is wonderful.
   - Everybody, what's another way of saying **The new movie was wonderful?** (Signal.) *The new movie was fantastic.*

6. The next word is **pale.** When something is **pale,** it is whiter than normal.
   - Everybody, what's another way of saying **Her face was whiter than normal?** (Signal.) *Her face was pale.*

7. The next word is **ridiculous.** When something is **ridiculous,** it is really silly.
   - Everybody, what's another way of saying **The president's speech was really silly?** (Signal.) *The president's speech was ridiculous.*

EXERCISE 2   General Review

1. When you see a play or a concert, what do we call the people on the stage? (Call on individual students. Ideas: *Performers, actors, musicians.*)
   - What do we call the people who watch the play or concert? (Call on individual students. Ideas: *Audience, crowd.*)

2. What were the two states you read about in the Waldo story? (Call on a student. Idea: *Colorado and Utah.*)
   - Which direction do you drive to get from Colorado to Utah? (Call on a student. Idea: *West.*)

3. Pretend you're teaching a dog a simple trick. What do you do after the dog does the trick? (Call on a student. Idea: *Give the dog a reward.*)

4. Here's a rule: Heavier planets have more gravity.
   - Which planet is heavier, Jupiter or Earth? (Signal.) *Jupiter.*
   - So which planet has more gravity? (Signal.) *Jupiter.*

5. Here's another rule: The less gravity there is, the higher you can jump.
   - Where is there less gravity, on Jupiter or Earth? (Signal.) *On Earth.*
   - So where can you jump higher? (Signal.) *On Earth.*

6. What happens to people if there is no oxygen in the air? (Call on a student. Ideas: *They can't breathe; they die.*)

7. What do we call a mountain that is made from hot, flowing rock that comes from inside the earth? (Call on a student. Idea: *A volcano.*)

- What do we call the hot, flowing rock that comes out of volcanoes? (Call on a student. Idea: *Lava.*)

8. Everybody, find the picture on page 8 of your Student Book. ✔

- Which glass will make the highest ring? (Signal.) *Glass C.*

- Why will that glass make the highest ring? (Call on a student. Idea: *Because it has the least water.*)

EXERCISE 3   Passage Reading

---

1. Everybody, find the passage on page 9 of your Student Book. ✔

- You're going to read the passage out loud.

2. (Call on individual students to read several sentences each. Correct all decoding errors. When the students finish, present the following questions.)

3. What did Maria think of Waldo's food? (Call on a student. Idea: *She didn't like it.*)

- How would Waldo probably feel if Maria told him that she didn't like his food? (Call on a student. Idea: *Hurt.*)

4. How did the animals feel about Waldo's food? (Call on a student. Idea: *They loved it.*)

- How did the animals show that they liked the food? (Call on individual students. Ideas: *They howled and screeched; they looked into the kitchen.*)

5. What would the animals rather do, escape from the pet store or eat Waldo's food? (Call on a student. Idea: *Eat Waldo's food.*)

6. Everybody, did Waldo open the cat cages **before** or **after** he opened the bird cages? (Signal.) *After.*

7. Why did Waldo brush the birds away? (Call on a student. Idea: *He wanted to keep them away from the food.*)

Retesting the Students

After you have completed the remedial exercises, retest each student individually. To administer the retest, you will need the student's Student Book, a blank copy of the Student Book, and a red pencil. Test the student in a corner of the classroom, so that the other students will not overhear the testing. Give the student the blank copy of the Student Book. Say, Open the book to lesson 80. You're going to take this test again. Read each item aloud and tell me the answer.

Use the student's own Student Book to grade the retest. With the red pencil, mark each correct answer with a **C** and each incorrect answer with an **X.** Then count one point for each correct answer and write the new score at the bottom of the page. Finally, revise the Individual Skills Profile Chart by drawing an **X** over any items the student missed on the retest. The chart should now show which items the student missed on the initial test and which items the student missed on the retest.

All of the Individual Skills Profile Charts should now be completely filled in for lesson 80. Enter the students' final scores in the appropriate boxes on the Group Summary Chart.

Fluency: Rate/Accuracy

Administer the fluency checkout for lesson 80. For further instructions, see page 29.

Tested Skills and Concepts

The Lesson 80 Assessment measures student mastery of the following skills.

- answering literal questions (item 16)
- comprehending vocabulary definitions (item 3)
- drawing conclusions (item 7)
- identifying literal cause and effect (item 14)
- inferring a character's point of view (item 12)
- inferring causes and effects (items 5 and 8)
- interpreting a character's motives (item 11)
- making comparisons (items 4 and 6)
- memorizing science facts and rules (item 9)
- predicting a character's actions (item 13)
- sequencing events (item 15)
- using rules to predict outcomes (item 10)
- using vocabulary words in context (items 1–2)

Lesson 100

Administering the Assessment

The Lesson 100 Assessment should be administered after the students complete all work on lesson 100 and before they begin work on lesson 101. To administer the assessment, you will need a Student Book and a pencil for each student. Use the following script.

1. (Have the students clear their desks and make sure that each student has a pencil.)

2. You're going to take another test in your Student Book. Do not open the book until I tell you.

3. (Pass out the Student Books.)

4. Find the test for Lesson 100. ✔

• Answer all the items on the test. For each item, circle the letter of the correct answer.

• There is no time limit. When you are finished, close your Student Book and look up at me. Begin the test now.

Grading the Assessment

You can grade the tests yourself, or the students can grade their own tests. If the students grade their own tests, use the following script.

1. We're going to grade the test. I'll read the correct answer for each item.

• If the answer is correct, mark it with a **C.**

• If the answer is wrong, mark it with an **X.**

2. (Read the correct answers from the answer key.)

3. Count up the number of correct answers and enter the score at the bottom of the test. ✔

Answer Key

Lesson 100

For items 1–2, circle the letter of the answer that means the same thing as the underlined part.

1. The shopper wanted to <u>trade</u> the pants at the store.
   a. exchange ⓐ
   b. flail
   c. trail

2. The soccer players <u>walked slowly</u> behind the coach.
   a. grasped
   b. included
   c. trudged ⓒ

For items 3–16, circle the letter of the correct answer.

3. What do we call objects that can float?
   a. buoyant ⓐ
   b. gravity
   c. miserable

4. What do we call a person who does a job without pay?
   a. volunteer ⓐ
   b. veterinarian
   c. assistant

5. What is coral made of?
   a. Petrified ocean plants
   b. Underwater gems and minerals
   c. Skeletons of tiny animals ⓒ

6. Where is the pressure the greatest?
   a. On a beach
   b. Under the ocean ⓑ
   c. On top of a mountain

7. What will sled dogs do when their driver yells "Gee"?
   a. Turn left
   b. Turn right ⓑ
   c. Move forward

8. Why do deep places in the ocean have fewer plants than shallow places?
   a. Deep places have less light than shallow places. ⓐ
   b. Deep places have less water than shallow places.
   c. Deep places have more farmers than shallow places.

Look at the picture on page 11. Then answer items 9–10.

9. Which letter in the picture shows the swing dogs?
   a. A
   b. B ⓑ
   c. C

10. Which letter in the picture shows the wheel dogs?
    a. A
    b. C
    c. E ⓒ

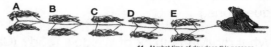

Read the passage below. Then answer items 11–16.

After school that day, Darla walked home with her sister Julie. Darla couldn't stop thinking about bravery. Finally, she asked her sister, "Am I brave?"

Her sister laughed and then shrugged. "I never thought about it," she answered. "I guess you are brave—at least in most things. But you sure are a sissy about going in the water."

"I know," Darla said. Then Darla added, "I'm really not very brave at all, because the things I do are pretty easy for me. Going in the water is different, though. If I just start thinking about it, I get scared."

"So you're a sissy about the water," Julie said. "You'll probably get over it."

Darla said, "If I were brave, I'd get over my fear of water right now."

Julie looked at Darla and the two girls fell into silence as they walked along the sidewalk. The sunshine was bright and warm. The girls walked for about a minute without saying anything. Suddenly, Darla stopped and said, "Julie, I've got to learn how to swim. I've got to be brave."

Julie smiled. "It's easy, Darla. The water won't bite you."

Darla said, "It's not easy for me. It's going to be the hardest thing I've ever done in my life. But I've decided that I won't like myself very much unless I'm brave."

Julie said, "I think they're going to give swimming lessons at the high school. I hear the instructor is very good."

Darla made a face. "Every time I think about it, I get scared. Feel the palms of my hands." The palms were sweaty. Darla said, "I'm scared. But I'll do it."

11. At what time of day does this passage probably take place?
    a. Afternoon ⓐ
    b. Morning
    c. Night

12. What problem did Darla have with water?
    a. She had trouble drinking it.
    b. She was afraid of it. ⓑ
    c. She was allergic to it.

13. How was Darla going to solve that problem?
    a. By taking swimming lessons ⓐ
    b. By going to the doctor
    c. By drinking milk

14. Why did Darla's palms become sweaty?
    a. She felt hot.
    b. She was afraid. ⓑ
    c. She wiped her face.

15. If Darla were brave, what would she do?
    a. Climb a mountain
    b. Learn how to swim ⓑ
    c. Ride a roller coaster

16. Where would Darla take lessons?
    a. At the public swimming pool
    b. At the grade school
    c. At the high school ⓒ

STOP - end of test - SCORE: _____

Recording Individual Results

Use the following script to record individual results.

1. (Distribute the Individual Skills Profile Chart.)

2. You're going to record your test results for lesson 100.
   - First look at the test and find out which items you got wrong. Then circle those items on the chart. I will help you if you have any questions. (Circulate among the students as they record their results.)

3. (After the students finish, say:) Count up the items that you did **not** circle and write the total in the **Total** box near the bottom of the column. The total should be the same as your test score. ✔

4. Now you'll fill in the other boxes for lesson 100.
   - If you scored 0 to 12 points, write an **X** in the **Retest** box.
   - If you scored 13 to 16 points, write your score in the **Final Score** box.

Remedial Exercises

Students who scored 0 to 12 points on the test should be given remedial help. After the regular reading period is over, assemble these students and present the following exercises. The students will need their Student Books.

EXERCISE 1 — Vocabulary Review

1. Let's talk about the meaning of some words.

2. The first word is **exchange.** When you **exchange** something, you trade it.
   - Everybody, what's another way of saying **The kids traded baseball cards?** (Signal.) *The kids exchanged baseball cards.*

3. The next word is **flail.** When you **flail** your arms, you swing them around in all directions.
   - Everybody, what's another way of saying **The players swung their arms around in all directions?** (Signal.) *The players flailed their arms.*

4. The next word is **trail.** When something **trails,** it follows behind something else.
   - Everybody, what's another way of saying **The ducklings followed behind their mother?** (Signal.) *The ducklings trailed their mother.*

5. The next word is **grasp.** When you **grasp** something, you grab it and hold onto it.
   - Everybody, what's another way of saying **The camper grabbed the ax and held onto it?** (Signal.) *The camper grasped the ax.*

6. The next word is **include.** When you **include** something, you let it inside something else.
   - Everybody, what's another way of saying **The family let the dog inside their plans?** (Signal.) *The family included the dog in their plans.*

7. The last word is **trudge.** When you **trudge,** you walk slowly.
   - Everybody, what's another way of saying **The girl walked slowly through the snow?** (Signal.) *The girl trudged through the snow.*

EXERCISE 2 — General Review

1. When something is **buoyant,** what can it do? (Call on a student. Idea: *Float on water or air.*)

2. How much do you get paid when you **volunteer** to do a job? (Call on a student. Idea: *Nothing.*)

3. You learned about a material that is made from the skeletons of tiny animals. What is that material called? (Call on a student. Idea: *Coral.*)

4. Where do you feel less pressure, on top of a mountain or at the bottom of a mountain? (Call on a student. Idea: *On top of a mountain.*)
   - Why do you feel less pressure on top of a mountain? (Call on a student. Idea: *Because there is less air above you.*)

5. When do plants usually grow better: when they have more light or when they have less light? (Call on a student. Idea: *When they have more light.*)

6. Let's review what you've learned about sled dogs.
   - What do we call the dogs at the front of the pack? (Call on a student. Idea: *Lead dogs.*)
   - What do we call the dogs right behind the lead dogs? (Call on a student. Idea: *Swing dogs.*)
   - What do we call the dogs right in front of the sled? (Call on a student. Idea: *Wheel dogs.*)

7. What command do you give if you want the sled dogs to turn left? (Call on a student. Idea: *Haw.*)

- What command do you give for turning right? (Call on a student. Idea: *Gee.*)

- What command do you give for starting the sled? (Call on a student. Idea: *Mush.*)

EXERCISE 3   Passage Reading

1. Everybody, find the passage on page 11 of your Student Book. ✔

- You're going to read the passage out loud.

2. (Call on individual students to read several sentences each. Correct all decoding errors. When the students finish, present the following questions.)

3. At what time of day does school usually get out? (Call on a student. Idea: *In the afternoon.*)

- So when would Darla and Julie walk home from school? (Call on a student. Idea: *In the afternoon.*)

4. What was Darla afraid of? (Call on a student. Idea: *Water.*)

- How did Darla went to get rid of her fear? (Call on a student. Idea: *By taking swimming lessons.*)

5. Was Darla brave about most things? (Call on a student. Idea: *Yes.*)

- What was she not brave about? (Call on a student. Idea: *Swimming.*)

6. What was Darla going to do at the high school? (Call on a student. Idea: *Take swimming lessons.*)

7. What happens to a person's body when that person gets really scared? (Call on individual students. Ideas: *Knees feel weak; teeth chatter; palms sweat.*)

Retesting the Students

After you have completed the remedial exercises, retest each student individually. To administer the retest, you will need the student's Student Book, a blank copy of the Student Book, and a red pencil. Test the student in a corner of the classroom, so that the other students will not overhear the testing. Give the student the blank copy of the Student Book. Say,

Open the book to lesson 100. You're going to take this test again. Read each item aloud and tell me the answer.

Use the student's own Student Book to grade the retest. With the red pencil, mark each correct answer with a **C** and each incorrect answer with an **X.** Then count one point for each correct answer and write the new score at the bottom of the page. Finally, revise the Individual Skills Profile Chart by drawing an **X** over any items the student missed on the retest. The chart should now show which items the student missed on the initial test and which items the student missed on the retest.

All of the Individual Skills Profile Charts should now be completely filled in for lesson 100. Enter the students' final scores in the appropriate boxes on the Group Summary Chart.

Fluency: Rate/Accuracy

Administer the fluency checkout for lesson 100. For further instructions, see page 29.

Tested Skills and Concepts

The Lesson 100 Assessment measures student mastery of the following skills.

- answering literal questions (item 16)

- comprehending vocabulary definitions (items 3–4)

- distinguishing settings by features (item 6)

- drawing conclusions (item 8)

- evaluating problems and solutions (item 12–13)

- inferring story details and events (item 11)

- interpreting a character's feelings (item 14)

- interpreting diagrams (items 9–10)

- memorizing science facts and rules (item 5)

- predicting a character's actions (item 15)

- using rules to predict outcomes (item 7)

- using vocabulary words in context (items 1–2)

Lesson 120

Administering the Assessment

The Lesson 120 Assessment should be administered after the students complete all work on lesson 120 and before they begin work on lesson 121. To administer the assessment, you will need a Student Book and a pencil for each student. Use the following script.

1. (Have the students clear their desks and make sure that each student has a pencil.)

2. You're going to take another test in your Student Book. Do not open the book until I tell you.

3. (Pass out the Student Books.)

4. Find the test for Lesson 120. ✔
- Answer all the items on the test. For each item, circle the letter of the correct answer.
- There is no time limit. When you are finished, close your Student Book and look up at me. Begin the test now.

Grading the Assessment

You can grade the tests yourself, or the students can grade their own tests. If the students grade their own tests, use the following script.

1. We're going to grade the test. I'll read the correct answer for each item.
- If the answer is correct, mark it with a **C.**
- If the answer is wrong, mark it with an **X.**

2. (Read the correct answers from the answer key.)

3. Count up the number of correct answers and enter the score at the bottom of the test. ✔

Answer Key

Lesson 120

For items 1–2, circle the letter of the answer that means the same thing as the underlined word.

1. The city made a new park near downtown.
   a. vibrated
   b. created ⟵
   c. addressed

2. The worm squirmed in the dirt.
   a. wriggled ⟵
   b. decorated
   c. exclaimed

For items 3–16, circle the letter of the correct answer.

3. Which one of these is matter in the liquid form?
   a. Steam
   b. Steel
   c. Milk ⟵

4. What is the coldest form of any matter?
   a. Liquid
   b. Gas
   c. Solid ⟵

5. In which form of matter do molecules move the fastest?
   a. Liquid
   b. Gas ⟵
   c. Solid

6. What will happen when your biceps pulls?
   a. Your arm will bend. ⟵
   b. Your arm will straighten.
   c. Your leg will straighten.

7. How is the bottom of the ocean different from the top of the ocean?
   a. The bottom is wetter.
   b. The bottom has more pressure. ⟵
   c. The bottom has more fish.

8. What did the sign on the old man's door say?
   a. See Everything—Go Everywhere
   b. See Anything—Go Everywhere
   c. Go Anywhere—See Anything ⟵

9. What do we call a cloud made up of stars?
   a. Solar system
   b. Molecule
   c. Galaxy ⟵

10. What do we call objects you can see through?
    a. Transparent ⟵
    b. Triceps
    c. Thorough

Read the passage below. Then answer items 11–16.

After supper Al said to Angela, "Let's go for a walk. I want to tell you something." Al didn't want his mother to hear what he wanted to tell Angela. The air outside felt very cold.

As they walked along, Al said, "I asked the old man if I could take you with me on one of the trips. He said it was okay. So after school tomorrow, you come to the store with me and we can go anywhere you want. We can see anything in the whole solar system."

"Al, stop this nonsense," Angela said. "You had your joke about the molecules. Now stop kidding around."

"Angela, I'm not kidding. I'm as serious as I can be. Come on, just go to the store with me."

"Do you really expect me to believe there's an old man who can take people inside a grain of sand?"

"That's right," Al insisted. "And that's not all. He can take us to the stars. He can take us inside the sun or to the bottom of the ocean. He can take us anywhere."

"I'm not going to listen to any more of this nonsense."

Al grabbed his sister by the shoulders and faced her. The light from a streetlight was shining on her face. "Please," Al said. "Please go with me, just one time. It's not a joke. You don't have to believe me. Go with me to the store tomorrow. Would you do that much?"

Angela sighed and pushed Al away. "All right," she said. "I don't know why, but I'll do it."

11. Why did Al want to talk to Angela outside?
    a. He couldn't talk while the television was on.
    b. He didn't want his mother to hear what he had to say. ⟵
    c. It was too hot inside the house.

12. Why did Angela think that Al was joking?
    a. He was talking about things that seemed impossible. ⟵
    b. He was making fun of her.
    c. He was telling a long and funny story.

13. What was the first thing Al did?
    a. He asked Angela to go to the store with him.
    b. He asked Angela to go for a walk. ⟵
    c. He grabbed Angela by the shoulders.

14. What will Angela probably do on the next day?
    a. Tell her mother what Al had said
    b. Go to the store with Al ⟵
    c. Play a joke on Al

15. Why did Al grab Angela by the shoulders?
    a. He wanted to hurt her.
    b. He wanted to keep her from falling down.
    c. He wanted her to look at him. ⟵

16. What was shining on Angela's face?
    a. The moon
    b. A car's headlight
    c. A streetlight ⟵

STOP - end of test - SCORE: _____

Recording Individual Results

Use the following script to record individual results.

1. (Distribute the Individual Skills Profile Charts.)

2. You're going to record your test results for lesson 120.
   - First look at the test and find out which items you got wrong. Then circle those items on the chart. I will help you if you have any questions. (Circulate among the students as they record their results.)
3. (After the students finish, say:) Count up the items that you did **not** circle and write the total in the **Total** box near the bottom of the column. The total should be the same as your test score. ✔
4. Now you'll fill in the other boxes for lesson 120.
   - If you scored 0 to 12 points, write an **X** in the **Retest** box.
   - If you scored 13 to 16 points, write your score in the **Final Score** box.

Remedial Exercises

Students who scored 0 to 12 points on the test should be given remedial help. After the regular reading period is over, assemble these students and present the following exercises. The students will need their Student Books.

EXERCISE 1   Vocabulary Review

1. Let's talk about the meanings of some words.
2. The first word is **vibrate.** When something **vibrates,** it moves back and forth quickly.
   - Everybody, what's another way of saying **The string moved back and forth quickly?** (Signal.) *The string vibrated.*
3. The next word is **create.** When you **create** something, you make it.
   - Everybody, what's another way of saying **The painter made a mural?** (Signal.) *The painter created a mural.*
4. The next word is **addressed.** When something is **addressed** to you, it has your name and address on it.
   - Everybody, what's another way of saying **The package had Bill's name and address on it?** (Signal.) *The package was addressed to Bill.*

5. The next word is **decorated.** When you **decorate** something, you add things to make it look prettier.
   - Everybody, what's another way of saying **They added things to the cake to make it look prettier?** (Signal.) *They decorated the cake.*
6. The next word is **wriggle.** When you wriggle, you squirm and move in all directions.
   - Everybody, what's another way of saying **The puppy squirmed on the rug?** (Signal.) *The puppy wriggled on the rug.*
7. The last word is **exclaim**. When you **exclaim,** you say something as if it is very important.
   - Everybody, what's another way of saying **The actor says something as if it is very important?** (Signal.) *The actor exclaims.*

EXERCISE 2   General Review

1. What are the three forms of matter? (Call on a student. Idea: *Solid, liquid, gas.*)
   - Name some matter in the solid form. (Call on individual students. Ideas: *Rocks, grass, houses.*)
   - Name some matter in the liquid form. (Call on individual students. Ideas: *Milk, water, orange juice.*)
   - Name some matter in the gas form. (Call on individual students. Ideas: *Air, oxygen, steam.*)
2. Everybody, what is the hottest form of matter? (Signal.) *Gas.*
   - What is the next hottest form? (Signal.) *Liquid.*
   - What is the coldest form? (Signal.) *Solid.*
3. Here's a rule: When molecules get hotter, they move faster.
   - You know which form of matter is the hottest. So in which form do molecules move the fastest? (Signal.) *Gas.*
4. Which muscle is on the front of the upper arm? (Signal.) *The biceps.*
   - Which muscle is on the back of the upper arm? (Signal.) *The triceps.*
   - Which muscle straightens your arm? (Signal.) *The triceps.*
   - Which muscle bends your arm? (Signal.) *The biceps.*

5. Where is the pressure greater in the ocean, at the bottom or at the top? (Signal.) *At the bottom.*

6. Where did Al see the sign that said Go Anywhere—See Anything? (Call on a student. Idea: *On the old man's door.*)

EXERCISE 3   Passage Reading

1. Everybody, find the passage on page 12 of your Student Book. ✔
- You're going to read the passage out loud.

2. (Call on individual students to read several sentences each. Correct all decoding errors. When the students finish, present the following questions.)

3. Did Al want his mother to hear what he had to say to Angela? (Call on a student. Idea: *No.*)
- So where did Al talk to Angela? (Call on a student. Idea: *Outside.*)

4. Why didn't Angela believe that Al had been inside a grain of sand? (Call on a student. Idea: *Because it's impossible for a person to go inside a grain of sand.*)

5. Did Al grab Angela by the shoulders **before** or **after** he asked her to go for a walk? (Call on a student. Idea: *After.*)

6. What did Angela finally agree to do? (Call on a student. Idea: *Go to the store with Al.*)

7. What time of day was it when Al and Angela went walking? (Call on a student. Idea: *Night.*)
- How was Al able to see Angela's face? (Call on a student. Idea: *A streetlight was shining on her face.*)

Retesting the Students

After you have completed the remedial exercises, retest each student individually. To administer the retest, you will need the student's Student Book, a blank copy of the Student Book, and a red pencil. Test the student in a corner of the classroom, so that the other students will not overhear the testing. Give the student the blank copy of the Student Book. Say, Open the book to lesson 120. You're going to take this test again. Read each item aloud and tell me the answer.

Use the student's own Student Book to grade the retest. With the red pencil, mark each correct answer with a **C** and each incorrect answer with an **X.** Then count one point for each correct answer and write the new score at the bottom of the page. Finally, revise the Individual Skills Profile Chart by drawing an **X** over any items the student missed on the retest. The chart should now show which items the student missed on the initial test and which items the student missed on the retest.

All of the Individual Skills Profile Charts should now be completely filled in for lesson 120. Enter the students' final scores in the appropriate boxes on the Group Summary Chart.

Fluency: Rate/Accuracy

Administer the fluency checkout for lesson 120. For further instructions, see page 29.

Tested Skills and Concepts

The Lesson 120 Assessment measures student mastery of the following skills.

- answering literal questions (item 16)
- comprehending vocabulary definitions (items 9–10)
- inferring a character's point of view (item 12)
- inferring causes and effects (item 15)
- interpreting a character's motives (item 11)
- making comparisons (item 7)
- making predictions (item 14)
- memorizing science facts and rules (items 4–5)
- recalling details and events (item 8)
- sequencing events (item 13)
- using rules to classify objects (item 3)
- using rules to predict outcomes (item 6)
- using vocabulary words in context (items 1–2)

Lesson 140

Administering the Assessment

The Lesson 140 Assessment should be administered after the students complete all work on lesson 140. To administer the assessment, you will need a Student Book and a pencil for each student. Use the following script.

1. (Have the students clear their desks and make sure that each student has a pencil.)

2. You're going to take another test in your Student Book. Do not open the book until I tell you.

3. (Pass out the Student Books.)

4. Find the test for Lesson 140. ✔
- Answer all the items on the test. For each item, circle the letter of the correct answer.
- There is no time limit. When you are finished, close your Student Book and look up at me. Begin the test now.

Grading the Assessment

You can grade the tests yourself, or the students can grade their own tests. If the students grade their own tests, use the following script.

1. We're going to grade the test. I'll read the correct answer for each item.
- If the answer is correct, mark it with a **C.**
- If the answer is wrong, mark it with an **X.**

2. (Read the correct answers from the answer key.)

3. Count up the number of correct answers and enter the score at the bottom of the test. ✔

Answer Key

Lesson 140

For items 1–2, circle the letter of the answer that means the same thing as the underlined part.

1. The players didn't have their <u>usual</u> coach today.
   - (a.) regular
   - b. suspended
   - c. terrific

2. She was <u>completely</u> certain she was right.
   - a. briskly
   - (b.) absolutely
   - c. chilly

For items 3–16, circle the letter of the correct answer.

3. Blood A is bright red. Blood B is dull red. Blood C is black. Which blood has the most oxygen?
   - (a.) A
   - b. B
   - c. C

4. Blood X has just turned bright red. Where would you find blood X?
   - a. In your arm
   - (b.) In your lungs
   - c. In your heart

5. What do we call the bundle of nerves that goes through the middle of your backbone?
   - a. Cerebrum
   - (b.) Spinal cord
   - c. Artery

6. Pretend you want to take a picture when it's very bright. What would you do with the iris of your camera?
   - a. Make it larger
   - b. Close it completely
   - (c.) Make it smaller

7. Some nerves tell your left hand how to move. Where do those nerves go?
   - a. From your left hand to your brain
   - (b.) From your brain to your left hand
   - c. From your right hand to your left hand

8. Where are you if it's night all winter long?
   - a. At the equator
   - b. In Mexico
   - (c.) At the North Pole

9. What do we call the part of your arm below the elbow?
   - (a.) Forearm
   - b. Triceps
   - c. Armband

10. What's another word for *pretty*?
   - a. Hollow
   - (b.) Attractive
   - c. Extended

Read the passage below. Then answer items 11–16.

Al, Angela, and the old man were in the library. Al and Angela were reading a book about the solar system. After they finished the book, the old man stood up and said, "How did you like this trip to the library? Did you like it as much as the trip we took to the bottom of the ocean?"

"No, I didn't," Al said. Angela agreed.

The old man said, "Did you like this trip as much as the trip to the poles or the trip through the human body?"

"No, I didn't," Al said.

The old man smiled. Then he said, "Taking a trip from a book is not as easy as taking a real trip. You have to use your imagination to take a trip from a book. You have to think hard about what you are reading."

The old man continued, "You can't go on real trips anymore. But you can still go back to the bottom of the sea by reading a book. And if you want to visit the other planets, you can take a trip from a book."

The old man stopped talking. The library was quiet. Al was thinking, "Maybe a trip from a book would not be as good as a real trip, but it would still be a good trip. It would be fun to take a trip to Africa. It would be fun to read about the Mesozoic era and Plateosaurus."

Slowly the walls of the library started to melt and everything started to become darker and darker. Al realized that they were back in the store.

The old man said, "I would like to shake your hands. I enjoyed the trips that we took together."

As the old man shook Al's hand, Al felt very sad. He wanted to say something to the old man, but he couldn't seem to talk. So he just nodded his head.

11. Which trip did Angela like the least?
   - a. The trip to the poles
   - b. The trip to the bottom of the ocean
   - (c.) The trip to the library

12. How is a trip from a book different from a real trip?
   - a. You need more time to take a trip from a book.
   - b. You need more money to take a trip from a book.
   - (c.) You need more imagination to take a trip from a book.

13. Why didn't Al say anything when the old man shook his hand?
   - (a.) Al felt sad.
   - b. Al didn't want to say anything.
   - c. Al was mad at the old man.

14. What will Al probably do if he wants to find out about rocket ships?
   - (a.) Read a book about rocket ships
   - b. Buy a ticket on a real rocket ship
   - c. Buy a toy rocket ship

15. What kind of animals did Al want to read about?
   - a. Monkeys
   - b. Fish
   - (c.) Dinosaurs

16. Why was Al sad?
   - a. He couldn't take any more trips from books.
   - (b.) He couldn't take any more trips with the old man.
   - c. He didn't like the trip to the library.

STOP - end of test - SCORE: _____

Recording Individual Results

Use the following script to record individual results.

1. (Distribute the Individual Skills Profile Chart.)

2. You're going to record your test results for lesson 140.
   - First look at the test and find out which items you got wrong. Then circle those items on the chart. I will help you if you have any questions. (Circulate among the students as they record their results.)

3. (After the students finish, say:) Count up the items that you did **not** circle and write the total in the **Total** box near the bottom of the column. The total should be the same as your test score. ✔

4. Now you'll fill in the other boxes for lesson 140.
   - If you scored 0 to 12 points, write an **X** in the **Retest** box.
   - If you scored 13 to 16 points, write your score in the **Final Score** box.

Remedial Exercises

Students who scored 0 to 12 points on the test should be given remedial help. After the regular reading period is over, assemble these students and present the following exercises. The students will need their Student Books.

EXERCISE 1   Vocabulary Review

1. Let's talk about the meanings of some words.

2. The first word is **regular.** When something is **regular,** it is usual or ordinary.
   - Everybody, what's another way of saying **Their usual routine never changed?** (Signal.) *Their regular routine never changed.*

3. The next word is **suspended.** When something is **suspended,** it is hanging.
   - Everybody, what's another way of saying **The light was hanging from the ceiling?** (Signal.) *The light was suspended from the ceiling.*

4. The next word is **terrific.** When something is **terrific,** it is wonderful.

- Everybody, what's another way of saying **The food was wonderful?** (Signal.) *The food was terrific.*

5. The next word is **briskly.** When you do something **briskly,** you do it quickly.
   - Everybody, what's another way of saying **They walked quickly?** (Signal.) *They walked briskly.*

6. The next word is **absolutely. Absolutely** is another word for **totally** or **completely.**
   - Everybody, what's another way of saying **They were completely thrilled?** (Signal.) *They were absolutely thrilled.*

7. The last word is **chilly.** When something is **chilly,** it is sort of cold.
   - Everybody, what's another way of saying **The air was sort of cold?** (Signal.) *The air was chilly.*

EXERCISE 2   General Review

1. What color is blood that has a lot of oxygen? (Call on a student. Idea: *Bright red.*)
   - What color is blood that has very little oxygen? (Call on a student. Ideas: *Black; dark.*)
   - In which part of your body does your blood get oxygen? (Call on a student. Idea: *In your lungs.*)

2. The iris controls how much light enters a camera.
   - What would you do if you wanted more light to enter the camera? (Call on a student. Idea: *Open the iris.*)
   - What would you do if you wanted less light to enter the camera? (Call on a student. Idea: *Close the iris.*)

3. Some nerves go from your feet to your brain. What do those nerves tell your brain? (Call on a student. Idea: *How your feet feel.*)
   - Some nerves go from your brain to your feet. What do those nerves tell your feet? (Call on a student. Idea: *How to move.*)

4. Why are the summer days so long at the North Pole? (Call on a student. Idea: *Because the sun never goes down.*)
   - Why are the winter nights so long at the North Pole? (Call on a student. Idea: *Because the sun never comes up.*)

5. When we say that someone is **attractive,** what does that mean? (Call on a student. Idea: *That they're pretty.*)

6. Where is your forearm? (Call on a student. Idea: *Below my elbow.*)

EXERCISE 3   Passage Reading

1. Everybody, find the passage on page 14 and 15 of your Student Book. ✔
- You're going to read the passage out loud.

2. (Call on individual students to read several sentences each. Correct all decoding errors. When the students finish, present the following questions.)

3. What did Angela like better, the trip to the poles or the trip to the library? (Call on a student. Idea: *The trip to the poles.*)

4. What do you have to use to take a trip from a book? (Call on a student. Idea: *Imagination.*)

5. What couldn't Al do any more? (Call on a student. Idea: *Take trips with the old man.*)
- So how did Al feel? (Call on a student. Idea: *Sad.*)

6. What will Al do now if he wants to find out about other planets? (Call on a student. Idea: *Read a book about planets.*)

Retesting the Students

After you have completed the remedial exercises, retest each student individually. To administer the retest, you will need the student's Student Book, a blank copy of the Student Book, and a red pencil. Test the student in a corner of the classroom, so that the other students will not overhear the testing. Give the student the blank copy of the Student Book. Say, Open the book to lesson 140. You're going to take this test again. Read each item aloud and tell me the answer.

Use the student's own Student Book to grade the retest. With the red pencil, mark each correct answer with a **C** and each incorrect answer with an **X.** Then count one point for each correct answer and write the new score at the bottom of the page. Finally, revise the Individual Skills Profile

Chart by drawing an **X** over any items the student missed on the retest. The chart should now show which items the student missed on the initial test and which items the student missed on the retest.

All of the Individual Skills Profile Charts should now be completely filled in for lesson 140. Enter the students' final scores in the appropriate boxes on the Group Summary Chart.

Fluency: Rate/Accuracy

Administer the fluency checkout for lesson 140. For further instructions, see page 29.

Tested Skills and Concepts

The Lesson 140 Assessment measures student mastery of the following skills.
- comprehending vocabulary definitions (items 9–10)
- distinguishing settings by features (item 8)
- drawing conclusions (item 4)
- identifying literal cause and effect (item 16)
- inferring a character's point of view (item 11)
- inferring story details and events (item 15)
- interpreting a character's feelings (item 13)
- making comparisons (item 12)
- memorizing science facts and rules (items 5 and 7)
- predicting a character's actions (item 14)
- using rules to classify objects (item 3)
- using rules to predict outcomes (item 6)
- using vocabulary words in context (items 1–2)

Fluency: Rate/Accuracy

The individual fluency checkouts measure decoding skills. For an individual fluency checkout, a student reads a passage aloud as you count decoding errors. Students earn points for reading the passage accurately. A fluency checkout takes about a minute and a half per student. Checkouts should be administered in a corner of the classroom so that the other students won't overhear.

Procedure

The student will read the passage for that lesson. The passage appears in the student's textbook in the lesson preceding the checkout lesson. For example, the passage for checkout lesson 10 appears in textbook lesson 9. Flower icons mark the beginning and end of the passages. The shaded portion in your answer key shows the words the student must read. The student may read further if able to. Use the following procedure.

1. Tell the student to look at the passage being assessed.

2. Note the time and tell the student to begin reading the passage.

3. As the student reads, make a tally mark on a sheet of paper for each decoding error the student makes. (See below for a complete description of decoding errors.)

4. At the end of one minute, tell the student to stop reading.

5. Record student performance as total time over number of errors in the appropriate box on the Individual Fluency: Rate/Accuracy Chart.

Decoding Error Guidelines

- If the student misreads a word, count one error.

- If the student omits a word ending, such as *s* or *ed,* count one error.

- If the student reads a word incorrectly and then correctly, count one error.

- If the student sounds out a word instead of reading it normally, count one error.

- If the student does not identify a word within three seconds, tell the student the word and count one error.

- If the student skips a word, count one error.

- If the student skips a line, point to the line and count one error.

- If the student does not finish the passage within the given time limit, count every word not read as an error. For example, if the student is eight words from the end of the passage at the end of the time limit, count eight errors.

Old Henry explained. "We are behind a lot of other | 10
geese. Those geese fly through the air and leave a trail | 21
of wind that moves in the same direction the geese are | 32
moving. We're flying through that air, so we don't have | 42
to work as hard as the geese up front." | 51

Tim said, "That's good for us, but I sure wouldn't want | 62
to be one of those geese up front." | 70

Henry said, "All the geese that are up front take turns | 81
at being the first goose in the V. They fly at the point for | 95
an hour or more and then change places with another | 105
goose." | 106

Then Henry noticed that his wing wasn't as sore as | 116
it had been. He hadn't been thinking about that wing | 126
because it hadn't been hurting. Henry realized that it | 135
hadn't been hurting because it didn't have to work as | 145
hard as it did when he and Tim flew alone. Henry said | 157
to himself, "If it doesn't get any harder than this, | 167
maybe..."He still wasn't sure how he would feel the | 177
next morning when the rest of the flock was ready to | 188
fly again. | 190

Later that afternoon, when the sky was starting to | 199
get very cloudy, the great V of geese went lower and | 210
lower through the clouds and came out of them above | 220
a beautiful green lake. Tim asked Henry, "What's that | 229
lake?" | 230

LESSON 15

As Oomoo stood near the great bear, she found it | **10**
hard to believe that this same bear used to fit inside | **21**
her jacket or that this bear used to sleep on the floor | **33**
of her winter home. | **37**
Usk had been Oomoo's friend for over two years, but | **47**
last fall something about him changed. He still liked to | **57**
play sometimes, but at other times he didn't seem to | **67**
be interested in Oomoo or in being with her. | **76**
Usk would go off by himself and walk along the high | **87**
slopes, sometimes howling into the air like a dog. | **96**

Sometimes he wouldn't come down to see Oomoo | **104**
for three or four days at a time. And each time | **115**
he came back, he didn't seem as playful as he had | **126**
been the time before. | **130**

One day late in the fall, another polar bear came | **140**
over the hills. It was a young male, about the same | **151**
size as Usk. Usk attacked that bear and drove it | **161**
away. That was the day that Oomoo's father told | **170**
her and Oolak not to go near the bear anymore. | **180**
"Usk is a bear," her father had told them. "And | **190**
bears do what bears do. They are not pets. Do not | **201**
go near Usk anymore. He could hurt you." | **209**

LESSON 20

Oolak looked very frightened and cold. His eyes were wide.   **10**
Oomoo tried to hold on to him and keep him from slipping off.   **23**
"Are we going to die?" he shouted.   **30**

"No, we're okay," Oomoo said. She was lying. She didn't   **40**
see any way that she and Oolak could survive.   **49**

Then suddenly the wind died. The waves still rolled and   **59**
continued to push the ice chunk beyond the floe. But the big wind   **72**
had stopped. Rain and hail started to fall. The rain and hail made   **85**
more noise than the wind had made. "Help!" Oomoo shouted.   **95**
But she was starting to lose her voice.   **103**

"Let's shout together," she said to Oolak. "One, two, three: **113**
help!" They repeated the shout again and again, until they could   **124**
not yell anymore. Still the rain and the hail pounded down. Even   **136**
though the rain was cold, it was much warmer than the ocean   **148**
water.   **149**

After half an hour, the rain began to die down. When the rain had   **163**
been coming down very hard, Oomoo had not been able to see more   **176**
than a few meters. Now she could see where they were. The ice chunk   **190**
was near the top of the C-shaped ice floe and it was still moving   **204**
north. Oomoo looked to the ocean, past the ice floe, and she could   **217**
see them—five or six of them.   **224**

Captain Parker was explaining the trip to the two girls. He   **11**
pointed to a map of Florida and the Atlantic Ocean as he spoke.   **24**

"We are starting from here," he said, pointing to the tip of   **36**
Florida. "We are going to follow this dotted line to an island   **48**
called Andros Island." Captain Parker continued, "That means   **56**
we will pass through a place where hundreds of ships have sunk   **68**
or been lost. It's called the Bermuda Triangle." Captain Parker   **78**
continued, "Many sailors say the Bermuda Triangle is the most   **88**
dangerous part of the ocean."   **93**

Carla's face seemed to drop.   **98**

"Hey," Captain Parker said, and smiled. "Nothing's going to   **107**
happen in a big ship like this. We are very safe. And this is not   **122**
the stormy season."   **125**

Carla asked, "Why is the Bermuda Triangle such a dangerous   **135**
part of the ocean?"   **139**

"Bad seas," the captain answered. "There are huge waves   **148**
and storms that come up without any warning. And there are   **159**
whirlpools."   **160**

Edna said, "You know what whirlpools are, don't you, Carla?"   **170**

LESSON 30

Edna said, "I don't think we should go into that jungle."   **11**

"Yeah, we shouldn't do it," Carla said. The girls were silent   **22**
for a few moments. They just stood there and looked at the great   **35**
path that led into the jungle. Then Carla said, "But we could   **47**
follow that path for a little way. We don't have to go too far."   **61**

"I don't want to go in there," Edna said. But she wasn't   **73**
telling Carla the truth. Part of her was frightened and wanted to   **85**
run away. But part of her wanted to see what made those huge   **98**
footprints. Her mind made pictures of that animal. In one of the   **110**
pictures, the animal was chasing Carla and Edna. Edna was   **120**
running as fast as she could, but the animal was getting closer   **132**
and closer and...   **135**

"Come on," Carla said. "Let's go just a little way."   **145**

Now another part of Edna's mind was taking over. It wanted   **156**
to see that animal. This part of Edna's mind was not terribly   **168**
frightened. It made up pictures of Carla and Edna sneaking up   **179**
on the animal. In these pictures, the animal did not see Edna and   **192**
Carla. "This animal is not very smart," Edna said to herself. "If it   **205**
was a smart animal, it would have found us last night. Maybe it   **218**
does not have a good sense of smell. Maybe it has poor eyes."   **231**

"I passed out, too," Edna said. Slowly, she turned around	10
and looked at the ocean. It was perfectly calm. She didn't see	22
any signs of whirlpools. And she didn't see any billowing clouds	33
that marked the island. "We must be far from the island," Edna	45
said.	46
Edna looked over the side of the boat, into the water. It was	59
very dark blue. She could see some fish swimming around	69
beneath the boat. They seemed to like staying in the	79
shadow of the boat. As Edna looked at the fish, she	90
remembered something she had once read. Fish have a lot of	101
fresh water in them. If you chew on raw fish, you can squeeze	114
the water out. Edna didn't like the idea of chewing on raw fish,	127
but she knew that without water, she and Carla would not last for	140
more than a few more hours in the hot sun.	150

Leonard was ready to forget about being an inventor. But | **10**
then something happened that changed the way he looked at the | **21**
problem. As he walked into the kitchen, he noticed that he had | **33**
mud on the bottom of his shoes. He hadn't noticed it before. Now | **46**
it was too late. He had made tracks all over the house. If only he | **61**
had noticed that his shoes were dirty. For a moment, he felt very | **74**
dumb for tracking mud all over the house. He could almost hear | **86**
what his mother was going to say: "You should always check | **97**
your shoes before coming into the house." | **104**

Leonard tiptoed over to the outside door and took off his | **115**
muddy shoes. He got some paper towels and started to clean up | **127**
the mess. Then, when he had almost cleaned the last footprint | **138**
on the kitchen floor, an idea hit him. It hit him so hard that it put a | **155**
smile on his face. Just like that, he knew how to think like an | **169**
inventor. He said out loud, "I need a shoe checker. I know I need | **183**
it because when I don't have one, I don't do a good job of | **197**
checking my shoes." | **200**

LESSON 45

He studied the arrow. He traced it with his pencil three or | **12**
four times. Then he traced over the letters in the sign. Then he | **25**
put two dots next to each other on the shaft of the arrow. | **38**
Suddenly he felt goose bumps all over his face and down his | **50**
back. He almost jumped out of his seat. "Wow!" he shouted. "I've | **62**
got it!" | **64**

Everybody in the class was looking at him. He could feel his | **76**
face becoming very hot. He cleared his throat and coughed. | **86**
Then he looked down at his paper. He could still feel the eyes of | **100**
everybody in the room looking at him. Then he heard the | **111**
teacher's voice. "Is anything wrong, Leonard?" | **117**

Leonard looked up. "No, no. I just figured out the solution to | **129**
a problem I've been working on." | **135**

The teacher said, "I'm glad to see that you are so excited | **147**
about solving your arithmetic problems, but when you work out | **157**
the solution to the next problem, try to be a little more quiet about | **171**
it." | **172**

LESSON 50

The man and woman approached Leonard's display. They   8
stopped. They didn't smile. They just stood there. "Hello,"   17
Leonard said at last.   21

The woman said, "Do you have a patent on this device?"   32
"Yes," Leonard replied.   35

The woman said nothing for a few moments. Then she said,   46
"I'm with ABC Home Products." The woman continued, "I don't   56
think many people would be interested in an invention like yours.   67
But I may be able to talk my boss into working out a deal. But   82
that deal must not involve a lot of money."   91

Grandmother Esther pointed to the large clock in the center   101
of the hall. "It's already after eleven o'clock," she announced   111
loudly. "This afternoon we're going to be very busy. This evening   122
we're going to win first prize and there will be many   133
manufacturers who are interested in this invention. If you want to   144
make a deal, you'd better start talking about a lot of money and   157
you'd better start right now."   162

LESSON 55

Wendy's mind moved away from the test. It began imagining 10
what it must be like to be in Traveler Four. Imagine sitting in a 24
comfortable passenger section that holds two hundred 31
passengers. Imagine sitting there, eating a snack and talking to the 42
person next to you as you streak through space at one thousand 54
miles each second. The idea was so strange and impossible and 65
exciting that Wendy could feel goose bumps forming on her arms. 76
Imagine going from Earth to Jupiter in only four-and-a-half days. In 87
that time, the spaceship would travel almost 400 million miles. 97
Imagine! 98

Suddenly, Wendy said to herself, "If you want to go on that 110
trip, you'd better do a good job on this test. So stop day- 123
dreaming and start working." 127

Wendy went back to the test. The next questions asked 137
about the planets in the solar system. The questions asked how 148
much they weighed, how fast they turned around, how long it 159
took them to circle the sun, how many moons they had and how 172
far from the sun they were. These questions were easy for 183
Wendy. She knew many facts about the planets. Of course, she 194
knew the most about the planet Earth. But the planet that 205
interested her most was Jupiter. Wendy found it interesting 214
because it was the biggest planet in the solar system. 224

After the exercises were completed, the flight attendants   **8**
served a big breakfast. As soon as the attendants started serving   **19**
the people in front of Wendy, she realized that she was very   **31**
hungry. Wendy ate her breakfast very fast. Sidney didn't eat her   **42**
roll, so she gave it to Wendy. "I don't know why I'm so hungry,"   **56**
Wendy said, "but I could eat a horse."   **64**

Wendy slept well that night. The next day she got up, did   **76**
her exercises, studied, ate lunch, studied   **82**
some more and took a nap in the afternoon. When she woke up,   **95**
the pilot was talking over the loudspeaker. She said, "We're   **105**
going to turn the spaceship sideways so that you can see Jupiter.   **117**
It is quite a sight."   **122**

Slowly, the ship turned. It continued to move in the same   **133**
direction it had been moving, but it was now moving sideways.   **144**
Wendy pressed close to the window. And there it was, the   **155**
largest planet in the solar system—Jupiter. It looked huge.   **165**
Wendy could clearly see seven moons. She knew that there   **175**
were 56 others, but she couldn't see them. The planet looked   **186**
like a great striped ball, with the stripes circling the planet. Some   **198**
stripes were dark brown, some were orange and some were   **208**
white. For a moment, Wendy couldn't talk. She heard the other   **219**
passengers saying things like, "Isn't that beautiful?" and   **227**
"Incredible!"   **228**

LESSON 65

Wendy sat down and realized that it was very hard to **11**
breathe. The harder she tried, the less she could breathe. She **22**
started to see spots in front of her eyes. Things were becoming **34**
purple and spotted. Her hands felt numb. She couldn't tell if she **46**
was sitting down or standing up. She wanted to cry. "Sidney," **57**
she said. "She's caught in the volcano. Help...her." She shook **67**
her head and tried to clear the spots away. Her hands and arms **80**
were covered with tingles. Her mouth was dry. She tried to **91**
swallow but she couldn't. She tried to talk but nothing **101**
happened. Her voice wasn't working. She started to see **110**
butterflies—purple ones. She... **114**

.   .   .

Wendy suddenly saw the shapes of people. "Help," she said. **124**
"Be quiet," a woman's voice said. Wendy realized that she **134**
was inside a vehicle that was bouncing over the surface of Io. **146**
Wendy's helmet was off. There was air inside the vehicle. Rod **157**
Samson was driving the vehicle. Another man was sitting next **167**
to him. A woman was in back with Wendy. The woman was **179**
attaching fresh oxygen tanks to Wendy's space suit. **187**

Waldo's first job was delivering newspapers. He didn't like   9
that job because he had to get up very early in the morning. The   23
second job that he got was cleaning up in a shoe store. He hated   37
that job. All he did was take boxes of shoes from the shelves and   51
dust the boxes. Then he would sweep the floor in the back room.   64
It was the most boring job in the world, but Waldo would have   77
kept that job if he hadn't found the third job. He would have kept   91
working in the shoe store because he liked earning money more   102
than he hated dusting boxes. So he dusted boxes and dusted   113
boxes and dusted boxes. The box dusting went on for two weeks.   125

Then, one day after work, he was walking home thinking   135
about what a terrible job he had. Suddenly, he heard a dog   147
barking. He turned toward the barking and noticed that he was in   159
front of a pet shop. Waldo looked at the dog that was barking. He   173
said to himself, "I have seen that dog in my yard before." The   186
dog continued to bark. At last the owner of the pet store went   199
over to the dog's cage. "Stop that barking," the owner shouted.   210
But the dog didn't stop.   215

LESSON 75

On the following afternoon, Waldo had two parrots do tricks on a little swing. The   **15**
parrots did some amazing things. They held on to the swing with their beaks. They did   **31**
somersaults on the swing. One parrot stood on the head of the other parrot, and both   **47**
parrots did a giant somersault. Then one parrot held on to the tail feathers of the other   **64**
parrot and they spun around and around as the swing went back and forth. From time   **80**
to time, Waldo would toss a little bit of food to the parrots. They would catch the food   **98**
with their beaks.   **101**

Again the crowd went wild. Again Maria reminded the crowd that the pet shop   **115**
would put on a full show that Friday night at Samson High School. She reminded the   **131**
people to bring their friends and family. "Remember," she said, "The admission is only   **145**
$1.00."   **146**

.   .   .

Waldo looked at the people who were lined up outside Samson High School.   **159**
"Wow," he said. "I think they all brought their friends and their families." There was   **174**
a line of people that went all the way out to the sidewalk and halfway around the block.   **192**
Maria said to Waldo, "The show will start in less than an hour. So you'd better go   **209**
inside and start cooking your food."   **215**

Waldo went on to explain how he planned to complete the pyramid. He told her that **16**
he planned to train eight squirrels to stand on the four cats and sixteen pigeons to stand **33**
on the eight squirrels. Waldo concluded by saying, "The next time we put on a show, it **50**
will be the greatest animal show that anybody ever saw." **60**

Maria said, "I hope so. Every time I think of the first show we put on, I feel like **79**
dying." **80**

Waldo said, "It will be different next time." **88**

And he was right. **92**

.   .   .

The hall at Samson High School was packed again. For a week before the show, **107**
Maria and Waldo had shown some of the acts that would be in the show. Each day, **124**
outside the pet shop, they showed a different act. There was one that they didn't **139**
show—the upside-down pyramid. Waldo didn't want anybody to see this act before the **153**
show. **154**

Just like the first show at Samson High School, some people had come from thirty **169**
miles away to see the show. But Waldo didn't worry about cooking his special food **184**
this time, because all the animals had been trained to work for regular food. When **199**
Waldo trained animals for a new trick, he used his special food because the animals **214**
would do anything to get that food. So the animals that made the upside-down **228**
pyramid had started out with special food, but now they worked for regular food. So **243**
did all the other animals in Waldo's acts. **251**

LESSON 85

"Yes," Waldo said. "That's the best trick in the world." It was the   **13**
best trick in the world because it saved so many lives.   **24**

Waldo signaled the pigeons and they flew from the pyramid. The   **35**
squirrels jumped down, the cats jumped down, followed by the two   **46**
smaller dogs.   **48**

Within an hour, the brakes on the trailer and the truck were fixed,   **61**
and the truck continued on its way to Utah. A long line of cars followed   **76**
the trailer.   **78**

The show in Utah was a great success. The newspapers carried   **89**
stories about the experience that Waldo and Maria had in the Rocky   **101**
Mountains.   **102**

Waldo was very pleased with the show. But the show that he   **114**
remembered as the greatest one his animals ever did took place in a   **127**
trailer that was speeding down a mountain road.   **135**

She signaled her sister that they could go the rest of the way to 14
the surface. Up, up, through the clouds of bubbles. Up, all the way to 28
the surface. 30

As soon as Darla surfaced, she noticed the sounds of birds and the 43
splashing of water. Julie came up right beside her. Julie pushed her 55
mask back onto her forehead. "Wow!" she shouted. "We made it!" 66

Darla smiled as she pushed her mask back. "Yeah," she said. "Yeah." 78

Julie swam over and kissed Darla on the cheek. "Thanks," she said. 90
Darla hugged her sister. 94

In the distance, the diving boat was moving toward them, making 105
a row of white-capped waves. The girls waved and shouted, "Over 116
here!" Before the boat reached the girls, Julie said, "Well, I guess 128
you're the brave one. When I lost my air, I couldn't think. I just 142
panicked." 143

"I would have done the same thing," Darla said. "I was scared to 156
death." 157

Julie replied, "I'm sure glad you stopped me. I guess I didn't know 170
what I was doing. I just had to have air." 180

LESSON 95

Susie didn't ask Chad these questions. But she had a lot of   **12**
others, and she asked them—one after another as the truck drove to   **25**
the examination station. She was still asking questions as she and   **36**
Chad waited at the station while the dogs were being examined. A   **48**
veterinarian and three assistants were checking Chad's team. The   **57**
inside of the station was pretty cold because the dogs were more   **69**
comfortable in cold than they were in heated places. At last Susie asked   **82**
Chad her last question. "Why did you decide to run with sixteen   **94**
dogs?"   **95**

"Well," Chad said. "It was a tough decision. A team of sixteen   **107**
dogs is a headache even if they work well together. But I figured that I   **122**
would be better off with more dogs. In case something happens, we'll   **134**
still probably have enough dogs to finish the race."   **143**

"Well, I guess you could say that," Chad replied. "I was proud of 13
all the dogs, and Denali certainly did his share, maybe even more than his 27
share." 28

"He did as well as the older dogs, didn't he?" 38

"Yes, he did," Chad said. "And if it's all right with you, I'll want him 53
to be a regular wheel dog for next year's Iditarod." 63

"Well, sure," she said. "I wouldn't want you to go out there without 76
him. You need Denali." 80

So even before everybody had congratulated Chad on finishing the 90
race, he was making plans about next year's race. Part of the plans 103
included working with Siri Carlson. She planned to do summer training 114
with Chad and his team. And Susie got the idea that Chad and Siri 128
seemed to like each other more than they would if they were just 141
mushing buddies. 143

She was right. Two years later, Chad and Siri got married. And 155
Denali ran in six more Iditarods. The musher for the first five races 168
was Chad. The musher for the sixth race was Susie. 178

Al ate dinner with Angela and his mother. He watched television   **11**
after dinner. Then he went to bed, but he had trouble going to sleep.   **25**
He kept thinking about that strange store and that old man.   **36**

The next morning, Al left for school very early. He wanted to see   **49**
what his science book said about speed. He wanted to make sure that   **62**
he would pass the test and go on another trip with the old man.   **76**

When Al read about the speed of light, a funny thing happened. Al   **89**
had read about the speed of light before. And he had found it very   **103**
dull. But when he read about it now, it was very interesting.   **115**

Another funny thing happened later in the day. The teacher was   **126**
talking about sound. She asked the class, "Why do you think it is quiet   **140**
in a jet plane that is traveling 900 miles per hour?"   **151**

Al raised his hand to answer the question. Everybody looked at him   **163**
because Al never raised his hand in school and never answered   **174**
questions. The teacher called on Al. He said, "It's quiet in a jet because   **188**
the engines are behind the people in the plane. And the jet is going faster   **203**
than the sound of the engines. The sound of the engines is traveling a   **217**
mile every five seconds. But the jet is traveling faster than that."   **229**

"That's really interesting," Al said, looking above the top row of **11**
vibrating molecules. **13**

The old man continued, "These molecules are the same temperature **23**
as the room. If we make the grain of sand colder and colder, you will see a **40**
change in the molecules." **44**

"I don't understand," Al said. "These molecules are in the solid **55**
form of matter. The solid form of matter is the coldest form. So how **69**
could the molecules change if the matter gets colder? The molecules **80**
will still be in the solid form." **87**

The old man smiled. "I see that you are using the information you **100**
have learned. Good for you, my friend. And you are right. The **112**
molecules will remain in the solid form of matter, but watch what **124**
happens to them when the temperature gets lower than the **134**
temperature on Pluto." **137**

The old man said, "There is more to the ocean than pressure. So | **13**
let's go back down and see some of the other wonders of the ocean. But | **28**
before we do, I want you to think about what you have just seen. I | **43**
want you to remember how the balloon changed. And I want you | **55**
to understand why it changed." The old man stopped talking. | **65**

Al thought very hard. He remembered the rule: The deeper | **75**
something is, the more pressure there is on that thing. He | **86**
remembered how the balloon got bigger and bigger when there was | **97**
less pressure on it. After a few moments, Al said, "I'll | **108**
remember everything." | **110**

"Me too," his sister said. | **115**

"Good," the old man said. "Now let's go back down and see some of | **129**
the wonders of the sea." | **134**

Al was ready to see them. Angela said, "That sounds great." | **145**

Al's mind felt heavy in school that day. It was too filled with facts and   **15**
thoughts about the things the old man had shown him. His mind was   **28**
so filled with information that he didn't feel as if he was ready to learn   **43**
more. In fact, he said, "Oh, no," to himself when his teacher announced   **56**
that on Monday the class would have a test on the human body.   **69**

Al didn't know much about the human body, and he really didn't   **81**
want to learn about it. And, he kept thinking about Christmas.   **92**

After school, he walked with Angela to Anywhere Street. They   **102**
walked down the street until they came to the store with the familiar   **115**
sign in the window. As soon as they entered, the old man stepped out of   **130**
the darkness. "Pay for your trip by passing a test," he said in a serious   **145**
voice. He fired questions at Al and Angela but they knew the answers.   **158**
They told him how big the large flames from the sun were. They told   **172**
him how much a spoonful of matter from the very old star weighed.   **185**

LESSON 125

The old man said, "A nerve is like an electric wire. It carries **13**
messages. This nerve goes from the hand to the man's brain. It carries **26**
messages from the hand." **30**

The old man continued, "Hold onto the nerve. You will see what **42**
kind of messages they are." **47**

Al and Angela touched the nerve. They could feel little pulses that felt **60**
like tiny electric shocks. Pulse, pulse, pulse, the nerve went. The **71**
pulses weren't strong enough to hurt. They felt like little trickles of **83**
electricity. **84**

The old man said, "You are feeling the messages that are **95**
coming from the man's hand right now. Watch what happens when the **107**
man starts to tie his shoe." **113**

Suddenly, the pulses started to go faster and faster. **122**

The old man said, "The man is feeling things. He is feeling the **135**
shoelace. He is feeling how his fingers move. And everything that **146**
he feels sends a message to the brain." **154**

The old man continued, "Those fast pulses are messages about **164**
everything the hand feels." **168**

Al responded by nodding his head yes. He went back to his desk, **13**
took out the book on the human body and started to read it again. **27**

As he was reading about the cerebrum, he noticed that the **38**
teacher was standing next to his desk. She said, "Al, here is your **51**
test. You got everything right. I have given that test for years and I **65**
don't remember anybody getting everything right before." **72**

The teacher told everybody their grades before school was out. Al got **84**
an A plus, the highest grade possible. Homer got a B. **95**

Al met Angela outside school, where he told her about the test. "I **108**
got every single answer correct," he said. "Imagine that. I never thought **120**
I would be smart in school, but I am smart." **130**

She said, "Oh, it was probably a very easy test." **140**
"No way," he said. "It was the hardest test you'll ever see." **152**

Then he continued, "Wait a minute. I have that test in my **164**
notebook. I'll bet you can't answer every question correctly." **173**

They stopped while Al flipped through his notebook until he found **184**
the test. Al pulled it out and said, "I'll read the questions. You tell me **199**
the answers." **201**

"We'll be back tomorrow to take the test," Angela said.   **10**

"Good," the old man replied.   **15**

Then the inside of the store grew very quiet. The old man had   **28**
disappeared.   **29**

"Let's go," Al said.   **33**

Angela opened the door. The bell went ding, ding. Outside, the snow   **45**
was very deep and new snow was starting to fall. The snow on the   **59**
sidewalk in front of the store was above Al's knees.   **69**

Angela said, "It's amazing to look at all this snow and realize that no   **83**
two snowflakes are exactly the same."   **89**

Al and Angela started wading through the snow to the corner   **100**
of Anywhere Street. And as soon as they went around the corner, Al could   **114**
hear the sound of Christmas songs and people on the sidewalk. Cars in   **127**
the street were moving very slowly through the   **135**
snow.   **136**

One car near the curb was stuck in the snow. The driver was trying to   **151**
move the car. "Wzzzzzz." The tires spun around and around, but the car   **164**
did not move forward.   **168**

The driver rolled down the window and called to Al and his   **180**
sister, "Can you give me a hand? I'm late and I've got to get home."   **195**

"Sure thing," Angela said.   **199**

As she and Al got behind the car, she said, "When I count to three,   **214**
push hard."   **216**

Angela made a snowball and threw it at the sign. When the	**12**
snowball hit the sign, the snow dropped off. Now they could read	**24**
the name on the sign. But the sign did not say ANYWHERE STREET.	**37**
It said ANDERSON STREET.	**41**
"I told you," their mother said. "There's no Anywhere Street in this	**53**
city."	**54**
Al shook his head. He didn't know what to say.	**64**
Slowly, Al and the others started to walk down Anderson Street. The	**76**
street looked a little different. Most of the stores on the street were	**89**
closed. But the old man's store was open. And so was the store next	**103**
to it.	**105**
Angela and Al stopped in front of the store next to the old man's store.	**120**
It had many different items in the window and on the shelves. And	**133**
there was a big sign in the window: GIFT SHOP—GIFTS FOR EVERYONE.	**146**
Al said, "Wow, that's strange! The other day..." Al didn't finish	**157**
the sentence.	**159**
Angela shrugged and smiled at Al. Then she said, "Look at the old	**172**
man's store."	**174**
Al ran over to the window of the old man's store. There were two big	**189**
signs in the window. One said GO ANYWHERE. SEE	**198**
ANYTHING—WITH BOOKS. The other sign said BOOKSTORE.	**206**
The inside of the store looked very bright. Al could see shelves	**218**
filled with books. And there was the old man sitting in a chair, reading a	**233**
book.	**234**

Interpreting Test Results

The test results are recorded on both the Individual Skills Profile Chart and the Group Summary Chart. Each chart gives a different interpretation of the results. The Individual Skills Profile Chart shows the specific skills that the students have mastered; the Group Summary Chart shows the group's overall performance.

Individual Skills Profile Chart

The Individual Skills Profile Chart should be used to assess each student's strengths and weaknesses. Test items that the student missed on an initial test will be circled; items missed on a retest will be crossed out. On the sample chart below, the student took a retest on lesson 60. Note that some items have been both circled and crossed out on lesson 60.

If a chart has more than 21 circled or crossed-out items, the student may still be weak in certain areas. Look for two general patterns of weakness. In the first pattern, a student will consistently fail items that measure a particular skill. On the sample chart below, for example, the student consistently failed items that measure "inferring causes and effects." Students who fall into this pattern may require further teaching of particular skills.

In the second pattern, a student will do poorly on one test but fairly well on the other tests. On the sample chart below, for example, the student did poorly on the test for lesson 60. Students who fall into this pattern may have been absent on the days preceding the test. These students may profit from a review of the lessons they missed.

Individual Skills Profile Chart

Skills	20	40	60	80	100	120	140
answering literal questions	11			16	16	16	
comprehending vocabulary	3	2	1	3	3	9	9
definitions	(4)	3	(2)		4	10	10
distinguishing settings by features	7				6		8
drawing conclusions		10	(16)	7	8		4
evaluating problems and solutions		5	3		12 / 13		
identifying literal cause and effect	12		(12)	14			16
identifying standard measurements	2						
inferring a character's point of view		16		12		12	11
inferring causes and effects	(5)	(12)		(5) (8)		(15)	
inferring story details and events		15	(11)		11		15
interpreting a character's feelings		13	15		14		13
interpreting a character's motives		11		11		(11)	
interpreting diagrams		6			9 / 10		
interpreting maps	9 / 10		(9) 10				
interpreting time lines			7 / 8				
making comparisons	14	(9)		4 / 6		7	12
making predictions	16		14			14	
memorizing science facts and rules	5 / 6	7 / 8	5 / 6	9	5	4 / 5	5 / 7
predicting a character's actions		14		13	15		14
recalling details and events	1		4			8	
sequencing events	13	1	13	15		13	
using rules to classify objects		4				3	(3)
using rules to predict outcomes	(8)			10	7	6	6
using vocabulary words in context				1 / 2	1 / 2	1 / 2	1 / 2
Total							
Retest							
FINAL SCORE							

Individual Skills Profile Chart

Skills	20	40	60	80	100	120	140
answering literal questions	11			16	16	16	
comprehending vocabulary	3	2	1	3	3	9	9
definitions	4	3	2		4	10	10
distinguishing settings by features	7				6		8
drawing conclusions		10	16	7	8		4
evaluating problems and solutions		5	3		12 13		
identifying literal cause and effect	12		12	14			16
identifying standard measurements	2						
inferring a character's point of view		16		12		12	11
inferring causes and effects	15	12		5 8		15	
inferring story details and events		15	11		11		15
interpreting a character's feelings		13	15		14		13
interpreting a character's motives		11		11		11	
interpreting diagrams		6			9 10		
interpreting maps	9 10		9 10				
interpreting time lines			7 8				
making comparisons	14	9		4 6		7	12
making predictions	16		14			14	
memorizing science facts and rules	5 6	7 8	5 6	9	5	4 5	5 7
predicting a character's actions		14		13	15		14
recalling details and events	1		4			8	
sequencing events	13	1	13	15		13	
using rules to classify objects		4				3	3
using rules to predict outcomes	8			10	7	6	6
using vocabulary words in context				1 2	1 2	1 2	1 2
Total							
Retest							
FINAL SCORE							

Group Summary Chart

Assessment	20	40	60	80	100	120	140
Number of assessment items	16	16	16	16	16	16	16

Notes for recording:

- Write student names in left hand column
- Record percent of items correct on each assessment and highlight a score below 80%
- Provide remediation to students with a score below 80%

Individual Fluency: Rate/Accuracy Chart

Student performance should be recorded as total time over number of errors.

Name	After Lesson Time/ #errors	10 1:00/ 2	15 1:00/ 2	20 1:00/ 2	25 1:00/ 2	30 1:00/ 2	35 1:00/ 2	40 1:00/ 2	45 1:00/ 2	50 1:00/ 2	55 1:00/ 2	60 1:00/ 2	65 1:00/ 2	70 1:00/ 2	75 1:00/ 2
Retest															
Retest															
Retest															
Retest															
Retest															
Retest															
Retest															
Retest															
Retest															
Retest															
Retest															
Retest															

Individual Fluency: Rate/Accuracy Chart

Student performance should be recorded as total time over number of errors.

Name	After Lesson Time/#errors	80 1:00/2	85 1:00/2	90 1:00/2	95 1:00/2	100 1:00/2	105 1:00/2	110 1:00/2	115 1:00/2	120 1:00/2	125 1:00/2	130 1:00/2	135 1:00/2	140 1:00/2	
Retest															
Retest															
Retest															
Retest															
Retest															
Retest															
Retest															
Retest															
Retest															
Retest															
Retest															
Retest															
Retest															

Placement Test

Part 1

1. California
2. Pacific
3. loudspeaker
4. lifeboat
5. Japan

"Fire! Fire!" a voice said over the loudspeaker. "The forward deck is on fire," the voice announced. "Everybody, leave the ship. Get into the lifeboats!"

Linda and her sister were on their way from the United States to Japan. Linda was thirteen years old, three years older than Kathy. Their father was in Japan, and they were on their way to visit him. Three days before, they had left California on a great ship called an ocean liner. They were now somewhere in the middle of the Pacific Ocean.

"Fire! Fire!" the voice shouted. "Everybody get into the lifeboats!"

People were running this way and that way on the deck of the ship. They were yelling and crying.

"Hold on to my hand," Linda said. The girls went to the lifeboats. People were all around them, shoving and yelling. Linda could not see much. She was afraid. Suddenly she was no longer holding Kathy's hand.

Suddenly a strong pair of arms grabbed Linda. "In you go," a voice said. A big man picked Linda up and put her in the lifeboat.

"Where's my sister?" Linda asked. Linda looked but she couldn't see her younger sister.

Part 2

1. Why was everybody trying to leave the ship? _____

2. Name the two sisters who were on the ship. _____

3. People were trying to get into the _____ .

4. Which sister was older? _____

5. How old was that girl? _____

6. How old was her sister? _____

7. Linda told Kathy, "Hold on to my _____ _____ .

8. When the big man picked up Linda, where did he put her? _____

9. What country were the girls going to? _____ _____

10. Why were the girls going there? _____ _____

11. How long had they been on the ship? _____ _____